MONDAY MORNINGS
with Stephenie

A Weekly Devotional for WOMEN

by STEPHENIE HANEY MONTES

MONDAY MORNINGS with Stephenie

A Weekly Devotional Book for Women

UnveiledRawMinistries@gmail.com

ISBN: 978-0-578-19074-7

Library of Congress In Publication Data

Category: Devotional, Christian, Inspirational, Motivational, Encouragement, Healing & Deliverance

Cover Design & Book Formatted by: Eli Blyden |
www.CrunchTimeGraphics.net

Printed in the United States by: www.PrintShopCentral.com

Special Thanks

To Jesus, who has given me the ability to write and to use it for Him so that I can help other women find refuge and strength in His arms. I am thankful for His grace and mercy and healing me from my past.

To my husband, Asbel, who is a huge support to my dreams and calling. He is a positive voice in my life and encourages me to push myself forward into doing my calling for God. He is a sound voice in my life, and for that I am appreciative. I love you so much!

To my late father, Kenneth Haney, whom I miss immensely and with whom I wish I could have a few more talks; he has taught me never to give up but to continue the course even when things get tough. He has taught me to keep plugging away no matter what is going on around me. He has taught me that it is important to show mercy to the fallen and to make everyone feels important regardless of his or her status in life.

To my mother, who is always there for me; she has taught me how to pray by example. Many (early) mornings growing up in our home, I would hear her in her prayer closet as she prayed for souls and situations that were out of her control. She taught me that faith is more than just a word but it is something that you have to put into action if you want to see the results. She taught me that sometimes fasting and prayer combined is necessary, and I watched her—without her announcing it—go on extended fasts and draw closer to God. She taught me how to speak life into situations I was struggling with. She and Dad were quite the couple who taught my siblings and me how to live for Christ. I am so thankful for both of them and for their influence in my life.

To my siblings: We've been through a lot together; we've laughed and cried together. We've encouraged each other through the ups and downs. I love you all so much.

To my editor, Bethany Sledge, thank you so much for taking time to edit my devotional book. I appreciate you so much.

A Note from Stephenie

My passion is helping women to overcome their pasts and their setbacks in life and to realize that they are important and matter to God. Women, you are more influential than you realize, so it is important for you to use your influence for something that is greater and bigger than yourself. We live in a world where there is a lot of suffering, pain and brokenness, and people need hope by knowing that they don't have to suffer alone. Jesus is our hope! At one time I thought I had let go of the hand of God and found myself running. But little did I know that there was an invisible hand keeping me. I had a mother and father praying for me and asking God to heal their daughter's heart that had been damaged and broken. I stand before you strong, not weak! I have learned that no matter what goes on in my life and no matter what situations come my way, I can lean on Christ to get me through it. You don't have to suffer alone; you don't have to go through life just barely getting by. You don't have to wear a mask and pretend for the rest of your life. You don't have to live insecurely and wonder what your purpose is. But you have a Father who cares for you. Give your hurts to Him. . . . Give the pieces of your heart to Him, and let Him make you whole again.

I pray that this weekly devotional book will inspire you to go for your dreams and to live a life full of faith and tenacity. I challenge you to dig deeper into the Bible and to find the golden nuggets there that can help heal your heart and also encourage you to keep on keeping on. It is time for women all over the world to pray, it is time to cover your home with prayer, it is time to fight the good fight, it is time to not give up, it is time to push yourself out, it is time to become bold and it is time to step into your calling and purpose and give 100 percent of your life to God.

Contents

WEEK ONE

Break the chains in your mind

Psalm 107:14: "He brought them out of darkness and the shadow of death, And broke their chains in pieces."

Oftentimes the chains have already fallen off and we've been healed, we've been restored and we've been given a second chance. But we are the ones still holding on to the past, pointing fingers, blaming others and keeping ourselves caged inside our minds.

I at one time allowed the wounds from my past to wrap chains around my mind. I even built a shrine around them and coddled each wound as if it were a trophy in my life. But they were destroying me! I had to come to the realization that I was never going to be free if I didn't take drastic measures and control my thoughts and the direction I had been going.

God had restored me, He had healed my heart yet I was still holding on to the chains that had me bound.

I was free, but I was still acting like I was in chains. I was still living in the past. I was still living in bondage because I was allowing my past to dictate to me my future. But one day I had had enough and took control over my life and thoughts and started speaking positive things into my life and getting rid of the clutter that I had allowed to build up inside my mind.

You can break the chains in your mind too, but you have to take control and stop letting your past control you!

1

I challenge you today to ask yourself, "What is holding me back?" What is controlling you that has brought a negative mind-set into your life? What do you need to break free of?

So today, it's time to break the chains that are in your mind.

John 8:31-32: "If you abide in My word, you are
My disciples indeed. And you shall know the truth,
and the truth shall make you free."

Don't allow the enemy to keep you bound inside your mind. Jesus is the way, the truth and the life, and He has set you free. Get into the Word and realize that you are no longer a prisoner of your past.

While Satan brings chaos, confusion and condemnation to your life, Jesus brings freedom and peace. Cling to Jesus instead of clinging to your past!

Date:_____

WEEK TWO
Be still, and know that I am God

How many times have we heard the verse of Scripture, "Be still, and know that I am God," and how many times have we told this to people who are going through difficult situations? How many times have we told ourselves that we too just needed to stand still?

Psalm 46:10: "Be still, and know that I am God."

Sometimes we can't be still physically because we have to navigate through life. But let me challenge you to "still" your thoughts.

Halt those thoughts that are racing and asking, "God, where are you?" or "I've been praying for so long, and I don't even see a sign from You that anything is happening" or "I am sick and tired of being sick and tired." Shhhh! Calm your thoughts.

I know these questions well, and sometimes I also wonder what is going on in my life and with the things I have been praying about. I get frustrated, I cry and I hurt too just like you. I have had a hard time as well trying to calm my thoughts when everything was unraveling around me. It is hard to "still" your thoughts when you or someone you care about has been diagnosed with cancer or something terminal. Maybe you are going through a divorce and you have no control over the outcome of it. Maybe you are jobless, and maybe you can't pay your rent or mortgage. These are a few of the many scenarios people are dealing with nowadays.

I implore you to take time this week to read Psalm 46 and pay close attention from the beginning to the end. I have to say, when it dawned on me what it was saying, tears flowed. It was a sign for me that God is still listening and that He sees where I am no matter what is going on in my life and around me.

Psalm 46:1: "God is our refuge and strength,
A very present help in trouble."
Psalm 46:11: "God . . . is our refuge."

No matter what type of hell has broken out in your life, He is your refuge! No matter what type of sickness and disease you are dealing with, He is your refuge! No matter who has walked out on you, He is your refuge! No matter what, He is your refuge! So while you are calming your thoughts, trying to be still and waiting on an answer while holding on for dear life, . . . be still.

Be still, and know that He is your refuge!

Psalm 46
God is our refuge and strength,
A very present help in trouble.
Therefore we will not fear,
Even though the earth be removed,
And though the mountains be carried into the midst of the sea;
Though its waters roar and be troubled,
Though the mountains shake with its swelling. Selah
There is a river whose streams shall make glad the city of God,
The holy place of the tabernacle of the Most High.
God is in the midst of her, she shall not be moved;
God shall help her, just at the break of dawn.
The nations raged, the kingdoms were moved;

He uttered His voice, the earth melted.
The LORD of hosts is with us;
The God of Jacob is our refuge. Selah
Come, behold the works of the LORD,
Who has made desolations in the earth.
He makes wars cease to the end of the earth;
He breaks the bow and cuts the spear in two;
He burns the chariot in the fire.
Be still, and know that I am God;
I will be exalted among the nations,
I will be exalted in the earth!
The LORD of hosts is with us;
The God of Jacob is our refuge. Selah

MONDAY MORNINGS with Stephenie

WEEK THREE

He is with you through
the ups and downs in life

Isaiah 43:2: "When you pass through the waters,
I will be with you;
And through the rivers, they shall not overflow you.
When you walk through the fire, you shall not be burned,
Nor shall the flame scorch you."

No matter what you will face in the future, He is with you. No matter what you are facing right now, He is with you. Hebrews 13:5 tells us that He will never leave us nor abandon us.

I remember when my father became ill, and as I sat there watching him, I sometimes felt frustrated that I was unable to control the situation. I felt like I was walking through the fire at times, and I have to admit that there were times I thought I might drown from the tears that flooded my heart and soul. I quoted all of the passages of Scripture I knew that would help bring me strength, but through the good, the bad and the ugly Isaiah 43:2 has become one of my favorite verses. I hold tight to it even when I am surrounded by the heat from the fire that is trying to pierce my soul. I cling to it even when sometimes the waters have overflowed my heart, trying to drown me in worry, fear and uncertainty. I continue to hold on to this Word. We have a promise in His Word that He will be with us through the waters no matter how high they may rise and through the fire no matter how intense it may get. He will never leave us or forsake us, and He is standing with us through every hardship that comes our way. He is with us through the thick and the thin.

So if you are feeling vulnerable,

If you are feeling fearful,

If you feel like you can't go another day with the situation that is bogging you down, don't forget that God is with you every step of the way. He's got this!

In Isaiah 41:10 the message version breaks it down for us like this. "Don't panic. I'm with you. There's no need to fear for I'm your God. I'll give you strength. I'll help you. I'll hold you steady, keep a firm grip on you."

We often call life a Roller Coaster ride and yes I have had my share of turning upside down, going through dark caves and the unknown. But God has always been there with me. He is there with you as you go through the ups and downs in life!

WEEK FOUR

It's okay to cry sometimes

Between the silence and the tears
God is still there.
Between the frustration and exhaustion
God is still there.
Between the betrayal and the rejection
God is still there.Between the diagnosis and the journey
God is still there.
Between the winter season and the spring season
God is still there.

Wherever you are and whatever you are facing, I can confidently say that God is right there with you every step of the way. I know what it feels like to face something that is out of your control and that is keeping you up at night. Your body is tired but your mind is wide awake as you pray over the situation you are dealing with. You thought you had run out of tears, but at 2 this morning, you felt yet again those hot tears running down your cheeks. It's okay to cry, allow yourself to feel . . . just know that God will be with you through the difficulties that come your way and that you can confide in Him and trust Him to do all things well. He will answer in His time, and He will come to your rescue. Psalm 107:19: "Then they cried out to the LORD in their trouble, And He saved them out of their distresses."

Sometimes you have to remove the mask and allow yourself to just cry. You go to work trying to escape the tears, and maybe you have been throwing yourself into the *staying busy* mode trying to avoid the raw emotions that are deep inside. Maybe you are hiding behind your children or spouse's life and are pushing them to excel, but behind closed doors when you're alone, the tears trickle down your face. Maybe you're single and you want so bad to fall in love with a guy who will love you back and treat you like a princess. Then you may be at a place where you feel stuck and in a place where you don't want to be. Regardless of where you are, just know that it's okay to cry sometimes and to allow yourself to be human. Tears have a voice, and they also speak to God.

He hears your tears, and He will calm your fears. Help is on the way!

Psalm 142 (Amplified)
I cry aloud with my voice to the LORD;
I make supplication with my voice to the LORD.
I pour out my complaint before Him; I declare my trouble before Him.
When my spirit was overwhelmed and weak within me [wrapped in darkness], You knew my path. In the way where I walk, They have hidden a trap for me.
Look to the right [the point of attack] and see; For there is no one who has regard for me [to act in my favor]. Escape has failed me and I have nowhere to run; No one cares about my life.
I cried out to You, O LORD; I said, "You are my refuge, My portion in the land of the living.
"Give attention to my cry, For I am brought very low; Rescue me from my persecutors, For they are stronger than I.
"Bring my soul out of prison (adversity), So that I may give thanks and praise Your name; The righteous will surround me [in triumph],
For You will look after me."

WEEK FIVE

Thy will be done

There are no *if's* in God's world. And no places that are safer than other places. The center of His will is our only safety — let us pray that we may always know it!"

— Corrie ten Boom

We all pray, "Lord, Your will be done." But is there a "but" at the end of our prayer? We females think we know what is best for our spouses, our children, our homes, our churches, our relationships, our own lives and our whatever's. But there are times that we have exhausted our resources and have to realize that it is out of our control. This doesn't mean we give up on people and a situation, but what we need to do is take a step back and pray, "Lord, Your will be done." You may be stressing over what is going on, but why not ask God to step in on your behalf and to do what His will is? That can be a difficult prayer sometimes to pray. "Lord, thy will be done in this situation," while the whole time we know what we want and how we want Him to do it. Are we trying to manipulate God to do it our way, or do we really mean what we are praying? He must chuckle sometimes with how we think or maybe He gets sad because of our lack of trust in Him. I could tell you story after story of some things I have experienced in my life where I tried to shove His will into my will. In my first marriage, God didn't restore it but He saved me instead. He brought me out of an abusive situation and into a new season. But it didn't come without pain, thorns and lots of scars, and even after I was out of that environment, I still was suffering with low self-esteem, a broken and wounded heart, and had lost my purpose in life. I was praying my will and then trying to force my will while telling God that He needed to fix it, but unfortunately it grew worse. I had to put my trust in Him and say, "Lord, Your will be done." My husband, Asbel, has a great quote that he says, "Sometimes God wants to be your Savior and not your Restorer." I didn't understand what God was doing during that season. I was a mess and frazzled, wondering what I was going to do with my life, but I now see that God did step in and He did save me.

James 4:13-15: "Come now, you who say, 'Today or tomorrow we will[g] go to such and such a city, spend a year there, buy and sell, and make a profit'; whereas you do not know what will happen tomorrow. For what is your life? It is even a vapor that appears for a little time and then vanishes away. Instead you ought to say, 'If the Lord wills, we shall live and do this or that.' "

We have to get to a place in life where we are submitted to whatever His plan is for our life. *His will is more important than our own will, plan and agenda.* Oftentimes I think we try to force His will to fit into our agenda, and that is just not how it works when it comes to God. This is about Him and His plan for our lives. He knows what is best for us.

When His will is being done, then nothing is being wasted.

Matthew 6:9-13
Our Father in heaven,
Hallowed be Your name.

Your kingdom come.
Your will be done
On earth as it is in heaven.

Give us this day our daily bread.

And forgive us our debts,
As we forgive our debtors.

And do not lead us into temptation,
But deliver us from the evil one.
For Yours is the kingdom and the power and the glory forever.
Amen.

MONDAY MORNINGS with Stephenie

Date:

WEEK SIX

Put down the sword and pray

Jesus went to the Mount of Olives, His disciples followed Him and there He prayed. In Luke 22 He told the disciples to pray so that they might not enter into temptation. He began to pray with intensity, knowing He was getting ready to go through much suffering, and said in verse 42, "Father, if it is your will, take this cup from me; nevertheless not My will, but Yours, be done." He then went to the disciples to check on them, and He found them asleep.

In verse 47 we are told that Judas brought the soldiers to Jesus and betrayed Him there. Then Peter took his sword and cut off the ear of the servant of the high priest, for he was ready to fight whoever he must to protect Jesus. But Jesus didn't hesitate, and instead he put the servant's ear back in place and healed him. You see, Jesus had been praying. He was in touch with something much more powerful than a physical battle that Peter could not get past because Peter was out of touch with God's will.

While I was reading this story, this quote came to me. "Put down your sword and pray."

Jesus was walking in the will of God. He had been praying and had surrendered His will even though He knew suffering was coming. But Peter was out of touch with the will of God; he had been sleeping while there was a call to prayer. Peter jumped on the bandwagon as so many of us do in this culture today, without even thinking what we say and what we do and the effect it will have on others. Peter wounded a man because he was out of touch with

God's plan and vision. Prayer brings calm and a reassurance even when someone is trying to wreak havoc on your life. Pray for wisdom when you feel the urge to retaliate. Don't force God to put the damage that your words and actions do to others back together. Seek His will first. Pray and then pray some more. If you are hurting and having a hard time understanding what is going on, then go ahead and let your tears speak for you. But through whatever it is that you are going through, just know that God is your calm in the midst of the storm. How often do we get in the way of the will of God because we are too busy slicing and dicing people and situations because we have not taken it to prayer first.

Today, I ask you to put down your sword and to pray. Yes, suffering hurts. And when we are hurting, it is easy to lash out at others, for oftentimes hurt people hurt people.

Find you a "mount of Olives" place to pray and surrender your hurts to God. If you are frustrated with what is going on in this world and in your personal world, don't take it out on others but take it to God. Don't try to make others pay for your pain, for Christ went to Calvary to heal your hurting heart. He bled and died on the cross so that you could receive your healing, peace and salvation. The next time you feel the urge to pull out the sword I challenge you to take the situation to Jesus first.

Psalm 141
LORD, I cry out to You;
Make haste to me!
Give ear to my voice when I cry out to You.
Let my prayer be set before You as incense,
The lifting up of my hands as the evening sacrifice.
Set a guard, O LORD, over my mouth;
Keep watch over the door of my lips.

Do not incline my heart to any evil thing,
To practice wicked works
With men who work iniquity;
And do not let me eat of their delicacies.
Let the righteous strike me;
It shall be a kindness.
And let him rebuke me;
It shall be as excellent oil;
Let my head not refuse it.
For still my prayer is against the deeds of the wicked.
Their judges are overthrown by the sides of the cliff,
And they hear my words, for they are sweet.
Our bones are scattered at the mouth of the grave,
As when one plows and breaks up the earth.
But my eyes are upon You, O GOD the Lord;
In You I take refuge;
Do not leave my soul destitute.
Keep me from the snares they have laid for me,
And from the traps of the workers of iniquity.
Let the wicked fall into their own nets,
While I escape safely.

WEEK SEVEN

Rise above it

The lotus flower is a beautiful flower that can be found all over the world. But the start of this flower's life is not as beautiful as one might imagine. It's unlike many other flowers. When the lotus first begins to sprout, it is under water, making its home in lakes and ponds in areas where the water remains fairly still on the surface. But underneath the surface, the lotus is surrounded by mud and muck and fish, by insects and simply dirty, rough conditions. Despite these conditions, the lotus flower maintains strength and pushes aside each of these dirty obstacles as it makes its way to clearer surfaces. At this time, the lotus is still just a stem with only a few leaves and a small flower pod. But in time, the stem continues to grow, and the pod slowly surfaces above the water, into the clean air, finally freeing itself from the harsh life conditions below. It is then that the lotus slowly opens each beautiful petal to the sun, basking in the worldly beauty surrounding it. The lotus flower is ready to take on the world. Despite being born into dark, murky conditions, where hope for such beautiful life seems dubious, the lotus grows and rises above adversity.

Even if you were born in poverty,

Even if you were born in a dysfunctional home,

Even if you have been dealt a deck of cards that has brought much heartache to your life,

Even if you are dealing with rejections, betrayals and difficulties, you can still flourish like the lotus flower. It is not over. It is not in vain. You will not stay in the murky waters forever. You will not be stuck in the mud forever, but you will rise above it!

You can and will get through the mud that you are currently covered in. No matter what we experience, God is growing us, stretching us and taking us to that place where He wants us to be.

There is purpose in everything! Let that sink in. Remember that God knows where you are and that He cares about you.

Matthew 10:29-31

"Are not two little sparrows sold for a copper coin? And not one of them falls to the ground apart from your Father's will. But even the very hairs of your head are all numbered. Do not fear therefore; you are more of more value than many sparrows."

You are more valuable than the lotus flower. Think about that for a moment. He sees and He knows. Stay close to God's unchanging hand.

The lotus flower didn't stay in its unfortunate circumstances forever but rose above it, and you can too. God is much bigger than what you are going through, so don't allow negative thoughts to take over your mind. Instead, start speaking faith into your circumstances. Even if you don't feel like it, do it!

Pray this with me.

"Jesus, help me to stop looking at my circumstances as a permanent situation, but help me to know that You, God, are much bigger than what I am going through. Thank You, Father, for forming me, for stretching me, for molding me and for believing in me. I know you are going to deliver me out of the muddy circumstances that I am currently in when it is time. In Jesus' name, amen."

WEEK EIGHT

Who is speaking into your life?

I Corinthians 15:33 "Do not be deceived: 'Evil company corrupts good habits.' "

Today, we have so many voices that speak into our lives on a daily basis. I'm not just talking about people but I am talking about social media, the news, internet, television, books and then, yes, the people who are in your life.

How many times have you read something online that brought on emotions of fear, anger and frustrations in you, and then you vented to everyone around you who would listen? Now, everyone knows you are upset, and you may even be one of those who goes and airs it all on social media and gets others riled up too. But how many times have you gotten worked up over nothing and then later you are mad at yourself because you wasted so much time on it? Stop doing it! It will become a vicious cycle, and you will continue to get drawn into it if you are not careful. I've learned that many voices are distractions and will take your focus off your priorities if you allow them to. Do not allow outside voices to come into your personal space, but protect it. Only you can protect it! If you do not have a strong network of sound and solid godly voices in your life, it is possible that you will find yourself sinking and maybe even self-destructing.

I believe strongly that we all need to be accountable to someone to help us stay on course. A lack of accountability can lead to bigger issues. That includes your walk with God, your business, your life, your dreams and your relationships. It is important to have a few safe people who are for you, who believe in you but who will also be honest with you and hold you accountable when necessary.

Don't allow just anyone to influence you.

Don't allow just anyone to come into your life and rearrange things.

Don't allow just anyone to tell you what God is calling you to do.

Don't allow bitter people to speak into your life.

Don't allow people who are shallow to speak into your life.

Don't allow people who are not praying and sensitive to God's voice to speak into your life.

Value your life. . . . Value the voices that you call "safe."

Value *you* enough to vet every voice that speaks into your life.

Your life is precious, so protect it and protect your home at all costs.

If someone gives you a word, tries to tell you what you need to do about a situation that you are involved in or if you read something that sounds off and it doesn't line up with the Bible, it is useless. Always test it. This is your life we are talking about, so don't be passive about it.

I John 4:1 (Amplified)
"Beloved, do not believe every spirit [speaking through a self-proclaimed prophet]; instead test the spirits to see whether they are from God, because many false prophets and teachers have gone out into the world."

WEEK NINE

Praying a hedge of protection

I grew up in a home where it was normal to hear people praying. My mother in particular woke up often very early in the morning to pray. It was a huge part of my life. But I remember hearing both my father and my mother saying, "I pray a hedge of protection around our family, around our church, around our children," and so on.

So I find myself often saying it too. Some of you may be asking, "What in the world does that mean?" I got to thinking about it and realized that some Christians may have never heard of this, and it is powerful! It is not just a bush full of thorns, but when you pray, you are praying for protection. I also believe that it is an act of faith to pray this. God can remove the hedge like He did in Job's life and gave Satan permission to destroy everyone close to him but Job. Job 1:10-12: " 'Have You not put a hedge [of protection] around him and his house and all that he has, on every side? You have blessed the work of his hands [and conferred prosperity and happiness upon him], and his possessions have increased in the land. But put forth Your hand now and touch (destroy) all that he has, and he will surely curse You to Your face.' Then the LORD said to Satan, 'Behold, all that Job has is in your power, only do not put your hand on the man himself.' So Satan departed from the presence of the LORD."

As you know, Job went through hell and lost everything but his wife. He lost his children and wealth and literally had nothing tangible to hold on to. He struggled greatly through this huge trial (that God allowed), but he did get through it.

Another story about the hedge of thorns and protection we find in the Book of Hosea. The prophet Hosea had a wife named Gomer who struggled with sensuality and infidelity. Hosea continued to try to keep her with him, but she would run into the arms of other men. One day God told Hosea that He would put a hedge of thorns in her way and keep her in so even if she pursued other lovers she would not find them. God put a hedge of protection around Gomer so she could not pursue the temptations that had been controlling her every move.

Hosea 2:6-7
"Therefore, behold, I will hedge up your way with thorns,
And wall her in,
So that she cannot find her paths.

She will chase her lovers,
But not overtake them;
Yes, she will seek them, but not find them.
Then she will say,
'I will go and return to my first husband,
For then it was better for me than now.' "

What have you been praying for? What are you desperate for? Do you have a family member who is a prodigal and running? Are you praying for your child or someone who needs God?

Maybe someone is sick in your family, maybe your business is struggling and maybe you just need a miracle right now!

Pray God will hedge them in and that they will go back to their first love, Jesus. Pray God will put a hedge of protection around your finances and bless them. Pray God will put a hedge of protection around your family and protect them from sickness, destruction, harm and danger. Pray God will put a hedge of protection around you, for we serve a God who answers prayer. Never give up praying for protection around your home and all those who are precious to you.

Psalm 91:11
"For He shall give His angels charge over you,
To keep you in all your ways."

WEEK TEN

Sometimes it's more than "just life"

John 10:10 (KJV): "The thief cometh not, but for to steal, and to kill, and to destroy: I am come that they might have life, and that they might have it more abundantly."

God has a plan, and the enemy is out in full force to ruin that plan. He wants to take your life and mess it up to the point that you cannot focus and do what you are called to do. He wants you to set your dream aside, to fall apart, to live in fear, to question the power of healing, to question the season you are in, to question what God is doing, to get you involved in dysfunction, to become wounded and jaded, to get you so busy that you have no time to pray and read the Bible. The enemy wants you to be a busybody about everybody else's business but your own. Distractions are his thing! He will use someone in your circle, at church or on the job to distract you and get you off course. Stay vigilant! Luke 22:31-32 tells us "And the Lord said, 'Simon, Simon! Indeed, Satan has asked for you, that he may sift you as wheat. But I have prayed for you, that your faith should not fail; and when you have returned to Me, strengthen your brethren.' "

The enemy wants you to stay in that rut of addiction, depression, insecurity, misery and negative speech. He wants you to remain broken; he wants you to be confused and focused on the wrong things. He doesn't want you to have a breakthrough because he knows the threat that you are to his plans. If you are all about God's kingdom and less about your kingdom, you are a threat to Satan's kingdom. He doesn't care if you build your kingdom up because that is what he did, and he knows what pride and the ego do to someone. He is a master at it! That is why we must continue to pray, "Create in me a clean heart; let my motives be right. This is about You, Lord, and what You want for my life. If I am prideful or making this about me, remove it, Lord, and forgive me for trying to raise myself up to being on Your level."

Perhaps you need to stop saying, "It's just life." Some things are *not* "just life." Discern! Discern! Discern! I've heard some say that their children were just going through normal teenage rebellion when in fact oftentimes there was a battle going on for their souls. Don't be passive about what is going on around you, for you may be the only one standing between them and eternity. Sometimes it's not "just life." Pray for God to reveal what is going on if you feel something is amiss. Be a Rahab, and stand up to protect your heart, your family, your dream, your calling and your home! In Joshua 2 we read that Joshua had sent two spies to her city to scope it out. The king of Jericho wanted to deal with the two spies, but she hid them and protected them. She told them that she knew their God was the God who had dried up the Red Sea, and she asked them to protect her family from the destruction that was coming to Jericho. Her family was spared from the destruction that came, but what I love about this story is that Rahab didn't follow the crowd in the city nor did she cower from doing what was right. But she recognized who these men were; she *discerned* that they were sent from the Almighty God, Jehovah. *Recognize what and who is in your inner circle and recognize what is going on around you.* First Peter 5:8: "Be sober [well balanced and self-disciplined], be alert and cautious at all times. That enemy of yours, the devil, prowls around like a roaring lion [fiercely hungry], seeking someone to devour."

Fight for sanity! Take authority! Sometimes you have to get bold and act like a mad woman and say, "I am not going to live in this any longer! I am better than this! I am a child of Jesus Christ! I have a purpose and I am not staying in this unhealthy place any longer! I am taking charge of my life today! I am writing a new chapter!" You have to call it like it is. Whatever you are facing today, call it out and take control! You have the power within, so do it! Jesus is greater than your dilemma! Satan trembles at the name of Jesus the Scriptures tell us in James 2:19. Call it out, and don't cower to it!

"You cannot defeat negativity if you do not address it
or call it out."

— Asbel Montes

WEEK ELEVEN

Walk away from drama

"Taking on too much of other people's drama is just a poor excuse
for not taking ownership and control over your own life."

— Jose N. Harris

I have quoted this many times, "If drama seems to be everywhere
you go, then it might not be the other person; it might be you."
You may want to dig a little deeper inside your heart to see if
you are the one creating the drama. I have been in contact with
people, including friends, who surround themselves with drama.
Everything is a huge deal, and they always seem to overreact over
even the slightest incident but are usually pointing the finger toward
someone else, blaming others for the drama and their reaction.

You have the choice to walk away from drama. . . . We all have
the choice to not get involved in it. Don't allow dysfunction to
become normal in your life. If you watch reality shows 24/7 where
they are screaming at each other and causing friction with other
people, then that might be another reason why you are functioning
in drama mode. You are what you feed on! It's unhealthy for you
and for your relationships. It is difficult to have peace when you are
living in chaos and speaking death and negativity into your life.
Walk away from it; you do not have to participate in it. Even if the
other party is yelling at you, upset or trying to discredit you because
you will not be a part of the scene they have created, you can still
walk away. I refuse to be a part of it. I was once involved in it, and

there was no peace! *You can't be a peaceful person if you are always creating drama.* I've been there, done that!

I wanted peace, but I had so much junk inside from my past that wasn't being dealt with that I found myself in the middle of drama. I kept pointing back to the one who had abused me and blamed him for why I was the way I was. But he wasn't keeping me there; I was keeping myself there. I had been away from it physically for a while, but I was still there emotionally. The lack of forgiveness and the abuse that I had gone through created a battered woman who acted out in a world full of drama. I got so sick of it though. Once I forgave and once I allowed Jesus Christ to heal my mind, my emotions and my heart, it stopped! I now walk away from drama, and I do not partake in it. I have no desire to get in the middle of it.

You don't have to enter every drama scene that comes your way; you can walk away from it. I'm at a place now where I am all about protecting my emotions, and I pray, "God, help me to not be a part of things that are unhealthy for me emotionally and spiritually." First Corinthians 14:33, "For God is not the author of confusion but of peace." I cannot go back to that life of drama; it was dysfunctional and affected me spiritually.

Protect your heart and your relationships. If you have children, don't let them think it's normal for people to scream and yell or call other people names. Don't let them think it is normal to sit around and talk bad about other people either. Get rid of the drama! Get rid of the negativity in your life! If you have to walk away from some relationships that are not good for you, then do it. You only have one life to live; don't live a life full of drama and negativity. You don't have to be hateful about distancing yourself either, but you do need to protect your mind and your home. Be kind but set some healthy boundaries.

If your middle name is *drama* you need to figure out why you thrive on it and go get the help you need so you can move forward into being a healthier you. Look in the mirror, face yourself and go from there. Lastly, find someone safe to talk to and get sound advice and let them hold you accountable while you work through these issues that have been controlling you. Sometimes when we are in the middle of drama we are not thinking clearly and our emotions are fragile. So having a safe person (someone in your inner circle, counselor, pastor or a family member) by your side can help you get through the chaos you find yourself in.

Proverbs 11:14 (Amplified): "Where there is no [wise, intelligent] guidance, the people fall [and go off course like a ship without a helm], But in the abundance of [wise and godly] counselors there is victory."

MONDAY MORNINGS with Stephenie

WEEK TWELVE

Stop trying to force it

*"I was trying to force something to fit into my heart,
but that particular piece didn't belong inside my heart."*

I look back to when I was a young and naive teenager; trying to
find my way, I fell in love. The guy wasn't the right fit for me,
but for some reason I thought that I could change him to fit into
my heart. My parents didn't think he was the right one for me either,
but what did they know? I mean, they were old-fashioned! They
didn't understand how I felt. This is what I would tell myself as I was
on a mission to force the pieces to fit. I was fixated on this mission,
and soon I would find out for myself that I just needed to walk away.
But the stubbornness in me refused to walk away. My parents tried to
warn me, but still I didn't listen. Have you ever wanted to just kick
yourself and rewind and redo some things? Yep, some things I wish I
could but I can't. I did learn a lot, though, through this lengthy lesson.
I learned that even when parents seem "too old-fashioned" with their
advice, there is some truth to it. Yes, my heart was broken, and I cried
and then I was upset because my parents were right and I didn't want
them to be right. They were trying to steer me away from getting my
heart broken, but I thought I knew more. It is important to listen to
people who have been through the cycle of life, for they can save you
some heartache if you will just listen.

What I learned through that is that you cannot force someone to
be a part of your life. You cannot force someone to love you, you

cannot force someone to care about you, and you cannot force someone to have good character and integrity. You cannot force someone to like peanut butter because you love it. You have to know when to let go. Some relationships are toxic and very unhealthy for your emotional well-being. You can try to cover up the toxins that are coming out and pretend they are not there, but they will be exposed again and again and again.

What are you trying to force to fit inside your heart but it doesn't belong there? It could be anything, from a relationship to a job or even a dream that is not the right dream for your life. I know that is hard to grasp, for I have had to give some of my dreams to God because they were my (personal) dreams and not in His plan. It was difficult for me to let go, but I know that if I am in His will, His dreams for my life will have more of an impact on people's lives than mine ever would. Now, to be quite honest with you, I didn't let go all that easily. It took me some time, but He has a way of prying it out of our hearts. I am now at a place where I pray, "God, don't let me force things into my heart that are not meant to be there." I don't want to play a role of getting in the way of where He is wanting to take me.

So wherever you are. . . . If you've been trying to force the pieces to fit and trying to force certain people to stay in your life, it is time to release them to God. No more forcing people, dreams, ministries and jobs to stay in your life. You can't force a square peg into a round hole; it's just not going to fit no matter how hard you try to force it to. Every person you meet and who has been a part of your life was for a purpose, but you cannot force someone to fit where he or she doesn't belong. It's like seasonal friends versus lifelong friends; sometimes we are guilty of trying to force a seasonal friend to become a lifelong friend. Some friends are meant to be with you for a season only and to help you get through that season. Well, some things and some people are not meant to fit into your *round hole* agenda, so let them go and trust God even when it hurts. Why do we sometimes try to force something if that person doesn't want it to begin with or if it's not meant to be? Girlfriend! Let it go! Give the pieces to God, give the people whom you have had a hard time letting go of to God, and He will put the pieces inside your heart that are meant to be there. He will take you to places you cannot even imagine when the right pieces are in sync with His plan for your life. Don't fight it, but trust in Him.

Proverbs 3:5-6 "Trust in the LORD with all your heart, and lean not on your own understanding; in all your ways acknowledge Him, and He shall direct your paths."

WEEK THIRTEEN

Do you need to change your perspective?

Today someone committed suicide.
Today someone brought a newborn into this life.
Today someone got bitter over a situation that involves family, church or business.
Today someone forgave, turned the other cheek and moved on.
Today someone filed for divorce.
Today someone was married.
Today someone is in need of food but there is none and their body is in starvation mode.
Today in America we have so many food options that we complain when we don't get what we want.
Today a child with leukemia is lying in a cancer ward wishing he could go outside and play.
Today a child is complaining that she has nothing to do and is bored.
Today someone was let go from his job and is now concerned as to how he is going to provide for his family.
Today someone got a promotion at her job and she is ecstatic about the future.
Today someone was told he has cancer and that there is nothing more the doctor can do.
Today someone was told that she is cancer free and her tears are tears of joy.
Today someone bought a beautiful new home.

Today someone lost their home.
Today someone was called "Beautiful."
Today someone was called "ugly."
Today someone experienced physical abuse but justified her partner's actions.
Today someone broke free from the mental and emotional connection she had with her abuser.
Today someone was told, "I hate you."
Today someone was told, "I love you."
Today someone is depressed because all she sees are the thorns in her life.
Today someone is thankful for life and sees the roses in spite of the thorns.
Today someone hoarded his blessings and is too selfish to give.
Today someone gave out of her sacrifice and not just her abundance.
Today someone took a risk and is flying high.
Today someone let fear get in the way of a great opportunity.
Today someone leaned on Jesus.
Today someone leaned on self.

"Life is no straight and easy corridor along which we travel free and unhampered, but a maze of passages, through which we must seek our way—now lost and confused, now checked in a blind alley. But always God will open a door for us, not perhaps one that we ourselves would ever have thought of, but one that will ultimately prove good for us."

— Joy Haney

It's tough, isn't it sometimes? We look at our lives, and many of us have gone through some hard times and have been challenged with our faith in God. You might be going through something pretty horrific right now, it's breaking your heart and you just want it to end like now! Perhaps the storm just passed over and you are finally breathing a sigh of relief as you clutch the Bible a little tighter to your chest, for you have learned to lean on Him, having gone through one of the most difficult times in your life.

Regardless of what you are going through, remember that someone else is going through something just as difficult and perhaps even more difficult. She may be at a place where she can barely keep her head above water, for she feels like she is drowning in life. Don't take life for granted, for everyday is a blessing.

There is a purpose for your life no matter where you are in it.

Try to see the lemonade being made with the lemons.

Try to see the roses that are attached to the thorns.

Try to see the door that is being opened no matter how slow the process seems to be taking

I have asked myself, "What can I learn from this?" and "What is God trying to show me and what is He trying to teach me?" I remember when I went through a really difficult time in my life about twelve years ago, and someone told me that God was trying to show me something through it. I didn't understand at that time how going through abuse was teaching me anything because I was angry and bitter and frustrated with my life. I am now at a place where my relationship with Him is more important than all of the curveballs that are thrown at me and the pain that I have had to face. I must trust Him with each day that He gives me, for we never know when He will call us home.

It is all about your perspective in life.

It is all about your perspective of who Jesus is in your life.

It is your perspective that will get you through life if you will allow it to.

Change your perspective, and watch what happens.

II Corinthians 4:18 "We do not look at the things which are seen, but at the things which are not seen. For the things which are seen are temporary, but the things which are not seen are eternal."

WEEK FOURTEEN

Never make a decision out of frustration

Sarah grew impatient with the will of God for her life, and out of frustration she forced something that brought havoc into her world. (Genesis 16 tells the story.) All this happened because she didn't wait for God's plan to fall into place. She got tired of waiting. She forced her will into God's plan and brought chaos and tension into her tribe.

Even when it seems like there is no movement occurring on the ground, there is still something moving and something stirring in a realm that we sometimes are not in tune with. If we are not careful, we can easily get distracted by what we are experiencing and grow tired of waiting for the promise. It is so important to pray before you make a decision when you are feeling frustrated. Let God give you clarity; allow Him to speak into your heart about your next move. He may want you to stand still and wait on Him or He may give you the green light to move forward into the next season, but whatever you do, make sure you are moving in the right direction.

In I Samuel 13 the story of King Saul is told. He was waiting on the prophet Samuel in Gilgal. But Saul grew impatient, he took the matter into his own hands, he put himself in Samuel's place and he offered the burnt offering. (It's a fascinating story about how important it is to wait on God before making an important decision.) First Samuel 13:13-14: "And Samuel said to Saul, 'You have done foolishly. You have not kept the commandment of the LORD your God, which He commanded you. For now the LORD would have established your kingdom over Israel forever. But now your kingdom shall not continue. The LORD has sought for Himself a man after His own heart, and the LORD has commanded him to be commander over His people, because you have not kept what the LORD commanded you.' " This act done by Saul is a symptom of what was in his heart and how he could not even wait a few more days or hours for Samuel to show up. It is imperative that you lean on God when making decisions for your life that can affect not only yourself but your family, company, church and relationships.

I know it can be difficult, for I have had to wait too, and there have been times when Asbel and I have prayed about a decision that we needed to make while we felt restless. We have had to encourage each other to continue to pray and wait. We've even fasted, seeking direction with some things that we knew had to have God in the middle of them, so we would avoid making a wrong decision. Honestly, there have been times I have said, "God, this is so easy for You, and all You have to do is this, this and this." But that is not how He works. I have learned that some decisions require much prayer so you will not act out of frustration while you are waiting.

There is nothing like that secure feeling you feel when you are trusting Him and moving inside His will. If there is no peace, that is a sign that you need to wait on Him and listen for His voice to give you direction. When the enemy brings confusion, you will not feel peace inside. But Jesus will give you peace even if you are feeling frustrated about what is going on in your life. There is absolutely nothing like the peace of God and knowing you are in His will even if it's not where you want to be. Let God give you that emotional peace and let Him calm your heart. First Peter 5:7: "Casting all your care upon Him, for He cares for you."

"Do not be anxious or worried about anything, but in everything [every circumstance and situation] by prayer and petition with thanksgiving, continue to make your [specific] requests known to God. And the peace of God [that peace which reassures the heart, that peace] which transcends all understanding, [that peace which] stands guard over your hearts and your minds in Christ Jesus [is yours]" (Philippians 4:6-7, Amplifed).

God's timing is always perfect, so wait to hear from Him when making an important decision for your life.

" 'For I know the plans I have for you,' declares the LORD, 'plans to prosper you and not to harm you, plans to give you hope and a future' " (Jeremiah 29:11, NIV).

WEEK FIFTEEN

God doesn't need our advice

Luke 8:17: "For nothing is secret that will not be revealed, nor anything hidden that will not be known and come to light."

There I am telling God what needs to be done. "Now, Jesus, I need You to do this, this and this, and then You need to take care of this person. He/she is on my last nerve. Then I need You to open this door like now! Oh, and, God, I cannot handle this, I'm about to lose it and I'm seriously going to have a meltdown. Please, just come on down here and fix it for me, and, God, You know they are lying about me, they are this and that? Please, just do something!" Sounds a bit comical? Well, how many times do we do this to God?

God doesn't need our advice or help on how to handle a situation, and He definitely isn't a genie in a bottle we can just order around as if we own Him. Let me be real clear here. He is going to handle it! He is going to do something about it! But the way He handles it will be in His time and in His own way.

It will be revealed when it needs to be revealed. Don't force His hand and don't rush His hand. In His timing He will take care of it. He sees the whole picture and knows exactly what is going on. Pray for wisdom, and continue to discern even when you feel you are between a rock and a hard place. He is in tune with what is going on in your life, so don't react out of frustration. He sees exactly what is going on; He is not blind to it. Sometimes it is difficult to understand what God is doing because everything seems to be falling apart or moving slow and it seems as if the situation is just getting worse and not better, but God will not put on you more than you can bear. He was with David when David was attacked by his elder; He was with Joseph when Joseph was lied about and when his integrity was in question. He was with Daniel when Daniel was facing the lions and had no place to run. But God revealed the truth and delivered all three of these men . . . in His time. A person's true character will be revealed in time. God always has the last say.

You also don't need to run around trying to convince people about the other person who has been bad-mouthing you or trying to expose their character, either. Let it go! God does all things well and He will take care of your situation. He always reveals the truth, but you can't rush the process and His timing. You will only frustrate yourself even more. Pray about this more than you are talking about it. There is power in prayer! God is always on time. Trust Him even when it seems like nothing is going on. Growing up, I watched my parents deal with some very critical situations that needed a major intervention. I watched them during times of a crisis where they took it to God and saw them pray and weep, asking God to step in on their behalf. I saw time and time again how God always came through for them. He always reveals the truth when He feels it's time. He will expose what needs to be exposed. He sees everything that goes on, so you might as well give it to Him and let Him take over. Time and time again I have seen God reveal what needs to be revealed in all types of situations because when He does it, He does it right. I have a friend who was dealing with a custody battle situation and the other party seemed to be a great role model, but she knew what was hidden. So she began to pray, and in time the facade fragmented and the truth was revealed. God is in charge, so you might as well take it to Him.

Daniel 2:22: "He reveals deep and secret things; He knows what is in the darkness, and light dwells with Him."

WEEK SIXTEEN

You are never alone

Hebrews 13:5: "For He Himself has said, 'I will never leave you nor forsake you.' "

Sometimes we do feel alone. Sometimes we wonder where God is.

Sometimes we feel like we are in the battle all by ourselves, warring for our home and the situation we find ourselves in. It is just the reality at times when we are standing in the gap and praying in our war room for the souls who are closest to our hearts. Then other times we just feel lonely and nothing we seem to do seems to shake off that feeling of loneliness.

I penned a song about this some time ago. Here are some of the lyrics.

"In the silence He will speak,
In the darkness He will be,
In the battle He will lead,
He will calm your raging sea."

I remember when I was a prodigal child running and wanted nothing to do with religion and church. I was a wounded soul needing refuge for my soul. I will never forget when I lived in Washington, DC, and was jaded with anything that had to do with Christianity. But during the night when I was alone, I would feel those hot tears running down my face and I felt so alone. I knew my parents were praying for me and praying that God would draw me to Him. It was during those lonely times when I still felt Him drawing me, and there I would remove my mask and let Him hold me. He never left me . . . I left Him. I also remember during the season of my life in DC that I had a good friend named Tonya who invited me to come stay with her family some weekends to get out of the city. She and her husband welcomed me with open arms in spite of where I was emotionally and spiritually. Some of my fondest memories are going to their home and spending quality time with them. They had no idea the loneliness that I felt during that time but they just showed me the love of Christ by being kind and showing mercy.

No matter where you are in life you are not alone. You may be married or even dating someone but you have this feeling of loneliness inside you. You may be a single mother trying to raise your kids right, you may be a single career woman working hard building your career, business and ministry but you feel lonely. At night you go home and sometimes will just pull out some ice cream or cookies and then cry because you feel lonely and find yourself eating out of emotion. I can honestly tell you that I have been where you are. I have eaten out of emotion and then would tell myself tomorrow would be a better day. Don't beat yourself up! These emotions come and go, but never think you are alone because you really are never alone! God is always by your side. Wherever you go, whether it be walking into church, into your job, into a special event or dinner hold, your head high because you are not alone!

Isaiah 41:10: "Fear not, for I am with you;
Be not dismayed, for I am your God.
I will strengthen you,
Yes, I will help you,
I will uphold you with My righteous right hand."

Between the silence and the tears
God is still there.
Between the frustration and exhaustion
God is still there.
Between the betrayal and the rejection
God is still there.
Between the diagnosis and the journey
God is still there.
Between the winter season and the spring season
God is still there.

Wherever you are and whatever you are facing, I can confidently say that God is right there with you every step of the way. I know what it feels like to face something that is out of your control and is keeping you up at night. Your body is tired but your mind is wide awake as you pray over the situation you are dealing with. You thought you had run out of tears, but in the wee hours of the morning, you feel yet again those hot tears running down your cheeks. It's okay to cry, to allow yourself to feel. But just know that God is your safe place and that you can confide in Him and trust Him to do all things well.

Psalm 142 (NKJV)
I cry out to the LORD with my voice;
With my voice to the LORD I make my supplication.

I pour out my complaint before Him;
I declare before Him my trouble.

When my spirit was overwhelmed within me,
Then You knew my path.
In the way in which I walk

They have secretly set a snare for me.

Look on my right hand and see,
For there is no one who acknowledges me;
Refuge has failed me;
No one cares for my soul.

I cried out to You, O LORD:
I said, "You are my refuge,
My portion in the land of the living.

Attend to my cry,
For I am brought very low;
Deliver me from my persecutors,
For they are stronger than I.

Bring my soul out of prison,
That I may praise Your name;
The righteous shall surround me,
For You shall deal bountifully with me.

WEEK SEVENTEEN

Only respond when necessary

"You'll never have control over other people's decisions, or what cards life deals you. Your power lies in the choosing of your response. That is the one thing you can control."

— John Mark Green

Proverbs 15:1-4
"A soft answer turns away wrath,
But a harsh word stirs up anger.
The tongue of the wise uses knowledge rightly,
But the mouth of fools pours forth foolishness."

This is probably one of the most challenging things for people in general to do: to know when to and when not to respond. But I have learned that in many cases the less you respond the more peaceful your life will be.

Only respond when necessary. There are times words are necessary and then there are times saying nothing is the best policy. It is important to pray for wisdom when handling difficult situations; in fact, pray for wisdom in all things. Knowing when to speak and knowing when to stay silent is a work in progress for most people (including myself).

Our words can heal or they can cause more damage. This week in your devotions take time to study James 3, where it talks about the tongue. It is a great study that will help guide you, and there are lots of hidden nuggets in there. Don't always feel that you have to be the one to have the last say and that you always have to prove your point. In the end, people are going to believe what they want to believe. When I was younger, in my early twenties, it was important to me for me to have the last say. I always had to prove my point. :-) But as I've gotten older and have a few life lessons tucked under my belt, I have come to realize that sometimes all I want to do is just to survive the storms that come my way, and the last thing on my mind is wanting to try to prove my point. People are going to talk regardless if you drown or if you stay alive. We all have the opportunity to speak or to stay silent, but knowing what to do in each situation is key!

When I was about twenty years old, I was sitting in my father's office at the church. I was distraught and upset, telling him about a horrible rumor that was going around about me. He just stayed calm and sat there. I told him that I was going to tell everyone who would listen that some so-and-so's started it and that they are just big liars and gossipers in the church! Oh, I was mad all right, and I wanted to go after them and tell them like it was! We had a big church too, so can you imagine me running around trying to stop the wildfire from spreading? :-) Oh, how young and naive I was! Dad finally spoke and told me to stand still and do nothing. That made me even more mad. I told him, "I can't just sit here and watch my reputation being destroyed." Then He said, "Let's pray." So we did. Do you know that I listened to my dad's words of wisdom and did nothing, and the rumor stopped? What if I would've made phone calls, went rushing around on a marathon trying to defend my innocence? That day God showed me that all I had to do was pray and trust Him.

So today in your own situation, how are you handling it? What are you going to do about it? We all have a choice with our words, so let's all pray for wisdom and let God guide us on this (sometimes) rocky journey called Life. If your situation is already on fire, maybe staying silent and praying is the best policy right now. I don't have all the answers, but I know a God who does. He does all things well, so pour your heart out to Him and let Him take care of the situation and the mess that you find yourself in.

James 1:19, Amplified: "Understand this, my beloved brothers and sisters. Let everyone be quick to hear [be a careful, thoughtful listener], slow to speak [a speaker of carefully chosen words and], slow to anger
[patient, reflective, forgiving],"

WEEK EIGHTEEN

It is well

I have often said that my mother reminds me of the Shunammite woman in the Bible. She speaks faith and life into every situation and has always said, "It is well," even when things didn't look well. She is someone I aspire to be like, and I am working towards implementing this phrase into my life more.

In II Kings 4 we find the story of the Shunammite woman and how the prophet Elisha promised her a son. She got her promise but then he died, and this is where I want to focus. She didn't wait for Elisha to come to her, but she saddled the donkey and took off to Mount Carmel, where Elisha was. He saw her coming from afar and told his servant to see what was going on and if everything was okay. So Gehazi went to her and asked if everything was fine, and she answered, "It is well." She held it together until she reached Elisha, and then she fell at his feet. The servant went to push her away but Elisha told him to leave her alone because she was a desperate woman. She told him her son had died but Elisha had promised her she would have a son. She wouldn't let go and she wouldn't stop until He did something about it. She was desperate, but she believed at the same time that it was well and that it was going to be okay. She took her miracle (her son) home with her.

Is it well in your life today? Are you struggling with believing and speaking faith?

Believe that your miracle is on its way.

Believe that God is going to step in and is going to meet your need.

Believe that God will breathe life back into your situation today.

Believe that no matter what happens in your life, He does all things well.

Believe that it is well today!

II Kings 4:25-26

"So it was, when the man of God saw her afar off, that he said to his servant Gehazi, 'Look, the Shunammite woman! Please run now to meet her, and say to her, "Is it well with you? Is it well with your husband? Is it well with the child?" ' And she answered, 'It is well.' "

Imagine this determined and desperate woman carrying her dead son and still saying, "It is well."

God knows what is best for you, and He will see you through. In Revelation 22:13 He tells us, "I am . . . the Beginning and the End." He knows what He is doing, so trust Him (even through your tears, disappointments, grief and pain). He is with you while you rejoice over your loved one being healed, and He is with you even when you are standing over a casket, having to say good-bye. He does all things well.

We must continue to say, "It is well," for He does all things well.

One day we will meet Him face to face, and maybe then some of the things that we don't understand now we will understand then. But until then, let us trust God with everything that happens in our lives and continue to say, "It is well."

WEEK NINETEEN

Don't twist the favor of God

Matthew 5:45: "That you may be sons of your Father in heaven: for He makes His sun rise on the evil and on the good, and sends rain on the just and on the unjust."

Don't twist the favor of God, don't question the favor of God, for He gives and He takes away.

1) Job was still favored even though he was being tested and put through a hellish trial, losing his family and estate all within a few hours. (His wife was the only one left in his family, and she was a negative voice in his life. He had no one to lean on while he went through his pain.)

2) David was favored even though he found himself hiding in caves and running from a man who was jealous and who made it known that he was going to destroy David. (David was anointed to be king. He was chosen by God but found himself hiding, depressed, full of anxiety, frustrated and running for his life.)

3) Paul was favored even though he was traveling on a ship to do God's work and became shipwrecked and stranded on an island. (Paul could've questioned God, "But, God, I'm your well-known minister who is taking the gospel to the world. How can You leave me stranded like this?")

These are just a few who went through hard times and experienced pain and struggled internally.

We equate popularity, big platforms and prestige that bring us glory as being highly favored by God. We can easily twist it all up, and we often do. I too am guilty of it. No matter where you are in life, you may be smack dab in the middle of a very difficult and painful situation! Just know that you are still favored! You are still His child, and He still has a plan for your life. Jeremiah 29:11 tells us that He knows the plans that He has for us, for us to prosper. In the end, God's favor can do what no power on earth can do! Remember, just because God's favor is on you does not mean that when trouble comes or bad things happen, His favor has left you. Psalm 5:12: "With favor You will surround him as with a shield." He is your shield in the time of your troubles, and His favor will take you through the many difficulties that you will come in contact with. He will be with you even when attacks from the enemy come your way. His favor protects you and will be that hedge around your family. His favor gives you discernment to know when you need to pray like you have never prayed before because there is an urgent situation going on. It's that still small voice that lets you know when something isn't as it appears. His favor picks you up when you are down, and His favor is "being with you" through some of your darkest nights. This is the other side of favor we don't hear about.

> Job 10:12: "You have granted me life and favor,
> And Your care has preserved my spirit."

No matter what happens in your life, just know that His favor will bring you victory through every test and trial that you experience. He is with you regardless if you are on the mountaintop or if you are in the valley barely hanging on. If you will lean on Him, He will give you strength to endure through the hard times. Don't let your expectations that being favored is all glamorous discourage you when something bad happens to you: when the doors don't open like you think they should or when someone stabs you in the back and does you wrong or when you find yourself in a desert and can't seem to hear from God. When you're battling cancer or maybe you feel like you are about to have a meltdown (emotionally) or maybe you are even in the middle of a divorce, it's breaking you. You thought you would be married forever. The thought of being alone again scares you, and now you wonder where God's favor is. Don't twist His favor, for we will all be tested as we go through life. Trust Him, for we serve a God who is with us through our pain and through our disappointments. You are still favored no matter where you are in life; stay close to God and His unchanging hand.

WEEK TWENTY

Depression doesn't have to be forever

In 2012 about seven months after my dad had died, I had a hard time shaking it off and I found myself in a deep depression. (We are told that 9.9 percent of Americans suffer with depression and the majority are women. These numbers are based on who has gone to the doctor for help, but how many are battling depression who have not gotten help?) I found myself at the bottom and in a dark place. I had no energy, nor did I care about climbing out of the dark web of depression that I found myself in. We all feel blah sometimes; even a few days into a week we can get into a funk but it usually doesn't last. But imagine feeling blah and in a funk for six months, then a year, two years and even four years and more. When Robin Williams, the popular comedian, committed suicide a few years ago, the whole world was in shock. *While he made the world laugh he was crying inside.* We are all so busy that we often fail to see this going on even in our inner circle or in our daily routine of going to work or to the gym, grocery store, school and even church. Daily we are passing depressed people who feel they have no way out. It's easy to hide for I hid it very well. I found myself not wanting to get dressed, and I just wanted to stay in my pajamas all day. I didn't care how I looked, and it took everything in me to make myself look decent when I went out of the house. My tears became my voice to Jesus, and the battle inside my mind was a horrific scene. But I can tell you that you do not have to live in a depressed mind-set forever. I believe you can get through it and that God can set you free! Depression will chip away at the foundation you are built on and make you feel like giving up on everything you believe in. It will cause you to shut down and make you feel like you have no purpose in life! But God is bigger than your depression! Everyone is going to feel depressed sometime in his or her life. "But are you going to stay there?" is the question. Many things cause depression. Broken relationships: Divorce, dating, a betrayal, broken relationships with a child or parent. Also the loss of a job, a career and even ministry. Grief: Losing someone and knowing that you will never see that one on earth again can cause a major low feeling to come into your life. Abuse: Emotional and physical, then the feelings of being rejected by the abuser. Those feelings create a vicious cycle when dealing with any form of abuse. Feeling stuck: You are ready for change and nothing is happening. Loneliness and just pure disappointments and setbacks in life. Deficiencies in your body can cause depression. Vitamin D deficiency, along with other health issues. I suggest talking to your doctor and getting lab work done to see if you have any deficiencies. Also, side effects from medication can cause depression and even suicidal thoughts. It can also be a chemical imbalance. Yes these things happen. Holistic medicine can be helpful, so if you can find a doctor who also believes in not just drugs to help with the symptoms but believes in natural remedies too, that is a great thing.

Satan also will zone in on your vulnerabilities and play with your emotions while you are down. Luke 22:31-32 (Amplified): "Simon, Simon (Peter), listen! Satan has demanded permission to sift [all of] you like grain; but I have prayed [especially] for you [Peter], that your faith [and confidence in Me] may not fail; and you, once you have turned back again [to Me], strengthen and support your brothers [in the faith]." Not all depression is a clinical issue and a chemical imbalance, but oftentimes depression is a spiritual thing and it must be fought with the Word of God. WHO (World Health

Organization) tells us that over $30 billion is spent by people trying to fix and deal with their depression annually. Think about that!

I believe that you do not have to live in it forever. David too struggled with depression and at times he seemed to be giving up! But he got through it. David said, "I am troubled, I am bowed down greatly; I go mourning all the day long. . . . I groan because of the turmoil of my heart" (Psalm 38:6, 8). But he didn't stay there forever, and you don't have to either! His story of overcoming pain, anxiety and depression is one we can read to encourage ourselves to continue the good fight. Get the help you need from a doctor if you are in a chronic depressed state of mind. Get some lab work done too. But lean on Jesus Christ to help you get through this thing called "depression" that you are experiencing. He is with you through it and will never leave you hanging on your own. He can totally set someone free from it; we do not have to live as depressed individuals feeling helpless and hopeless for the rest of our lives. Cling to the cross, and let Him heal your troubled mind. It is not God's will for us to live depressed, for He has given us hope and the tools to overcome it.

Deuteronomy 31:8: "And the LORD, He is the One who goes before you. He will be with you, He will not leave you nor forsake you; do not fear nor be dismayed."

Psalm 9:9: "The LORD also will be a refuge for the oppressed, A refuge in times of trouble."

MONDAY MORNINGS with Stephenie

WEEK TWENTY-ONE

Nothing is worth missing heaven over

I will never forget back in 2010 sitting in my parents' living room with my husband, Asbel, and listening to them talk about forgiveness. They told us about their journey and how important it had always been for them to forgive those who had hurt them. It was refreshing to hear the realness and the raw side of them as they took us down their personal road of forgiveness. They talked about how through the years in doing ministry offenses had come to them and tried to take them down, but they were determined always to forgive no matter what. They kept saying this phrase, "Nothing is worth missing heaven over." Looking back now, I know that night was a God moment for them to speak into our lives to help us get through our journey that sometimes brings offenses into our own lives too. Forgiveness seems to be such a popular subject in this culture since there are so many hurt people hurting other people. There are evil people in this world, there are people who are just out for themselves in this world, there are people who sow discord and have destroyed people's lives with their words and actions. Maybe you are one who has been hurt and wounded and maybe you are even struggling with a root of bitterness yourself.

I understand, for I have been bitter and have wanted to get even with those who have hurt me. After I experienced abuse I was bitter and angry and then I had to deal with other things that hurt me. But being bitter and unforgiving is a miserable place to be. I implore you to rethink your tactics and to surrender your pain to God and to forgive those who have hurt you. The Bible is very clear on forgiveness. If we do not forgive others, He will not forgive us. Matthew 6:14-15: "For if you forgive men their trespasses, your heavenly Father will also forgive you. But if you do not forgive men their trespasses, neither will your Father forgive your trespasses."

It is hard when the wound is fresh and still bloody from the knife that has been shoved in and twisted, causing us much pain. But I promise you that Jesus can give you peace through this if you will just forgive and let Him take care of those who have hurt you. I hurt for people who are bitter and who will not forgive, I guess because I have been where they are. But you cannot and will not ever be happy living in that mind-set of unforgiveness, and you cannot excel in God if you do not forgive. Stop letting people and situations from the past eat away at you, for they are holding you captive in your mind.

I ask you today, is what you are holding on to worth missing heaven over?

The Bible is very clear about forgiveness and how it is imperative for us all to have a clean heart. We cannot have a clean heart when we are holding on to past offenses and clinging to bitterness. You may be one who says, "I've moved on," yet you know in your heart that you haven't because you have not forgiven. I am asking you please to take some time today and maybe even this week to reexamine your heart and to release the things that you know have a hold on you. Be open, raw and real with Christ, and pour your heart out to Him.

Let it go. . . . Release it. . . . Let Him help you become free.

"To be a Christian means to forgive the inexcusable because God has forgiven the inexcusable in you."

— C. S. Lewis

WEEK TWENTY-TWO

He is the Father to the fatherless

In November 2011 my father was taken away. You see, Jesus had a plan that was different from my plan. My plan was for my dad to live forever and to be the sound voice in my life and security that I always looked to. But God ended my dad's assignment here on earth and said, "It's time to come home. You don't need to stress any more, Kenneth. You've built churches, you've reached out to souls around the world, you've helped restore broken people and fallen ministers, you've been my voice for decades and now I want you to rest and to come home and to prop your feet up and be with Me."

After he passed away I felt fatherless. I mean, who was going to be there for me like Daddy was? Who would be my elder; who would speak into my life like Daddy had? All these questions didn't help my broken heart during this season. You may have a similar story like mine and miss your daddy too.

In the past few years, I have thought about all of those who have never experienced a father like mine and those who may have never known who their father was. Some may have been abused by their father or may have an estranged relationship with their father. They long to have a father who loves them and who can be a steady voice in their life. As I look around our broken world I see so much dysfunction and friction in relationships and in families. In many of these cases it's because the father figure is missing, but that is where Jesus comes in. You see, He can be our earthly Father too just like He is our heavenly Father if we will let Him. I struggled with this concept for a while because I wanted my daddy back. I was a little perturbed with my heavenly Father for taking away my earthly father. But I soon realized that Jesus wanted me to start allowing Him to be my soundboard in situations when I needed Daddy. He wanted me to cry to him when I was missing my (earthly) daddy. He wanted me to seek Him for advice and for reassurance.

Did your father pass away too? Do you miss him like I do sometimes? Do you still struggle sometimes with the loss?

Are you one who has never known your father? Maybe he abused you? Maybe he is in prison? Maybe he left you and your mother when you were a little girl and you wonder why he never loved you or took time out for you. You might still have many questions about your childhood, and the life that you have lived.

Life is sad sometimes.

We all hurt sometimes.

We all come from different walks.

You may be on the other side of the tracks from what I've experienced but we still have one thing in common; that is, we both hurt because we miss the presence of an earthly father.

Allow Jesus to fill the void in your life. I got to a place where I had to release the pain and other emotions that I was feeling because I had been refusing to let go. Jesus wants to be there for us. He wants to hold us. He wants to wipe our tears with His nail-scarred hands. He wants to caress our broken hearts and disappointments. So let's let Him. He created us so He already knows what we are thinking inside.

Give him your daddy and let him fill that void.

He is the Father to the fatherless, so let Him be your earthly and heavenly Father. I ask that all of us will show mercy to those who hurting and who are in need of a father. Be compassionate and let them know that Jesus can fill the void in their lives today.

Psalm 68:4-6
Sing to God, sing praises to His name;
Extol Him who rides on the clouds,[a]
By His name YAH,
And rejoice before Him.
A father of the fatherless, a defender of widows,
s God in His holy habitation.
God sets the solitary in families;
He brings out those who are bound into prosperity;
But the rebellious dwell in a dry land.

WEEK TWENTY-THREE

Guard your heart

Song of Solomon 2:15: "Catch us the foxes,
The little foxes that spoil the vines,
For our vines have tender grapes."

The South American vine called *matador* is a vine that begins at the foot of a tree. It slowly works its way to the top. But as it grows, it kills the tree. Matador means "killer."

What you are tolerating may seem harmless while it's just a "small" thing, but if it is allowed to grow, it will clasp itself around your heart and eventually kill the soul!

What you allow to take root will eventually spread and spiritually contaminate your heart.

Protect your heart.
Protect your family.
Protect your dreams.
Protect your passions.
Protect your relationships.
Protect your home.
Protect your calling.
Protect your soul.

The saying, "Focus on the majors, not the minors," I agree with to a certain point. But if all of us would focus more on some of the minors that we think are insignificant, we wouldn't be dealing with some of the major issues in our life today.

Many times we see the red flags and we know something is off, but we are all guilty sometimes of ignoring it and need to be paying more attention to it. We avoid confrontation because we don't want to hurt someone and we definitely don't want to deal with a situation that will turn into drama and chaos. (I get it; I really do.) But usually later on it's grown into something much bigger and has started controlling the environment in which we live, all because we wouldn't nip it in the bud when we saw the first red flag. I am guilty of having done this before and excusing someone's behavior thinking it would just go away, but it didn't. In fact, it got worse. Don't be afraid to confront something if necessary. You don't have to be hateful about it but you can handle it gracefully and be firm at the same time. The vine will continue to grow and the foxes will continue to destroy the vines if you do not handle the necessary things in a timely manner.

I think we can all ask ourselves these questions: What am I scared of? What stops me from dealing with it?

It can be scary when dealing with people who are controlling or those who talk to you as if you are beneath them. But you just hurt yourself when you don't address it and push it under the rug. This can apply to anything. Your home may be a war zone and you have allowed it to get there because you have tried to bite your tongue and have been walking on eggshells for a while now. I understand trying to diffuse the chaos and not wanting it to escalate, but you can't live walking on eggshells for the rest of your life either. Maybe you are dealing with a situation at your job and now it's to the point where you dread going to work because it has escalated. Wherever it is that you have allowed yourself to become a doormat to others, it is time to stop letting the foxes play in your vineyard, it's time to stand up with dignity and it's time to throw the eggshells away and walk with your head held high with confidence. Some of the small battles we are ignoring are worth fighting because if we don't, we take the risk of them growing into a battle that is beyond our control. Turn a new leaf today and start fresh. You can do this! Be alert and guard your heart and don't allow the little things to grow and to destroy everything you've worked hard for. Stand up!

"Guard your heart above all else, for it determines the course of your life" (Proverbs 4:23, NLT).

WEEK TWENTY-FOUR

Is fear choosing your destiny?

"Fear herds us into a prison and slams the doors. Wouldn't it be great to walk out?"

– Max Lucid

Are you allowing fear to choose your destiny? Fear comes in all forms. I have struggled with fear too. It will keep us in a prison inside our own mind if we don't confront it.

I don't believe in embracing your fear; the more you coddle it the worse it becomes. Don't let your fears lead you and guide you; instead, allow the Word of God and Jesus Christ to lead and guide you away from those unhealthy fears.

Here is a list of some fears people in general tend to have:

• Fear of disease

• Fear that God will take someone you love away from you to live with Him

• Fear of losing your job

• Fear that people won't like you if you step out and do something different

• Fear of divorce

• Fear of being single for the rest of your life

• Fear of falling in love again

• Fear of the unknown

• Fear of rejection

- Fear that people are talking about you
- Fear of heights
- Fear of flying
- Fear of animals
- Fear of water
- Fear of speaking in front of people
- Fear of failure
- Fear of not accomplishing a dream before you die
- Fear of darkness
- Fear of crowds
- Fear of intimacy
- Fear of commitment
- Fear of the future

There are many reasons why a person fears. This is a small list compared to all of the things that people do fear in this world. Some are scared of commitment because they have already been down that road and gave their heart away only to feel the backlash of betrayal, so now they run from commitment. Fear often paralyzes a person to the point that she will not do something if it involves the thing that she fears. There is a big difference between actually fearing something and not doing something because it's just something you don't want to do. For instance, I have no desire to skydive. Is it something I fear? Actually, I never think about it; it's just something that I have no desire to do. It is definitely not on my bucket list to do, and it's not going to cause my destiny to go haywire if I do not fall from the sky.

Of the above list of fears, I have probably experienced a few of them at some time in my life.

According to the National Institute of Mental Health, 10 percent of Americans suffer with some kind of phobia. But how many more suffer with a phobia and just haven't seen a doctor about it? We are surrounded by crazy and chaotic situations that are often out of our control; and the news networks are constantly feeding our fears and making it worse. I am of the belief that there are a lot more out there who have just learned how to cope with their phobias. Phobia is just another name for fear. Phobia comes from the Greek, *phobos*, which means fear.

When fear steps into your mind, what do you do? How do you handle it? Do you start entertaining those thoughts of fear and the "what ifs", and then the spirit of doom also steps into your mind?

"The mind is where the battle lies." – Dad (something I probably heard my dad say one hundred times a year)

Maybe this will help relieve you to know that you are absolutely not alone out here in this flawed world.

David experienced fear. He was scared of King Saul. Even though he knew that he was anointed by God to be the next king, he still ran and hid.

Peter experienced fear. He had tons of faith and started walking on the water, but then common sense set in and he began to fear.

Jonah experienced fear. Even though God put him in the whale and spoke to him, he still had fear.

In I Kings 19 we read about Elijah the prophet who ran scared because Jezebel threatened to take his life, but in the chapter before this we read how God had just used Elijah in a supernatural way. He had called fire from heaven and had killed 450 false prophets to show who the real God was, Jehovah. But then a chapter later we see Elijah running scared.

So don't beat yourself up for fearing something, but at the same time, do not let it keep you there! Do not let your fear drown you, suffocate you and stop you from fulfilling a dream or stop you from fulfilling the call that Jesus has placed on your life. If anything, let that fear that tries to stop you put the will in you to fight! It is not over! Keep on keeping on!

There is one person I know whose faith in God has always outweighed her fears, and it's been this way since I was a little girl. That person is my mother! She has this incredible faith that I have never seen in anyone else. I don't care what is going on or how devastating the news is; she always speaks faith into the atmosphere. I watched as my father was not doing well in fall 2011, but she continued to speak faith until God took him home. She never wavered, nor did she even plan a funeral and start making arrangements even when the naysayers gave their opinions and had him in the grave before his time. She still believed that God would raise Dad up until the end. But I watched my mother look fear in the eye and say, "God is my God, He is in charge of the situation. You will not control me, fear!"

A challenge to us all today: Take control of the fear that has consumed you and that has taken you down the road away from your dreams and purpose. As Kirk Franklin says in one of his songs, "Hello, Fear!" I'm saying "Hello" and "Goodbye" to fear today!

Isaiah 35:4: "Be strong, do not fear! Behold your God . . . will come and save you."

Acts 18:9-10 declares: "The Lord spoke to Paul in the night by a vision, 'Do not be afraid, but speak, and do not keep silent; for I am with you."

Matthew 28:20 gives us confidence as Jesus spoke: "I am with you always."

"Do not let your fears choose your destiny"
– Unknown

WEEK TWENTY-FIVE

There is purpose through the process

We are all shaped by our experiences in our lives. There is purpose through the process. The process you are going through is developing you for the next phase and next season in your life.

A few years ago Asbel and I were talking to a group of women at the Unveiled Conference about going through the process, and for a moment the real me came out and I said, "Hang the process." Everyone started laughing, but seriously, that is how I feel sometimes. But regardless of how I feel, God is going to continue the process, so I might as well get into the seat, put my seatbelt on and just go with it.

We humans can be so fickle at times, though. We pray and ask God, "Please do this and that," and sometimes even beg Jesus to open certain doors, to give us favor and to use us. We tell God that it is our dream and passion and that we want so much for it to happen. "Please make a way!" But when we start experiencing difficulties, pain, betrayals and suffering, we then are begging God to step in and stop it because we hate going through the process. Are we confused with what we want, or do we just not want to go through the process because it requires too much of us and it takes way too much time to go through it? Do we just want to wave a magic wand and then everything that we have been praying for is right there sitting right in our laps, and then we will know that we have arrived?

We want the diamonds but we don't want to go through the process to get them. We just want them handed to us on a silver platter.

There is a new attitude in America that used to not be here. Many want free handouts and expect just to have everything handed to them on a silver platter without having to work for it or are not willing to sacrifice their lifestyle for it. They just think it's owed to them. It's a new mentality that has come into this country. If we are not careful, we can have this same attitude with God. We just expect Him to give us anything we want without sacrifice, tests, suffering or trials. If you look through the Bible, most everyone paid some sort of price and sacrificed or was tested before he got his diamonds in life.

- Abraham was tested as to whether or not he was willing to give up his only son.

- Joseph was sold into slavery in a foreign country, then lied on and went to prison for something that he didn't even do. But after all he went through, he then was promoted to a big position in Egypt.

- Sarah had to wait decades before she gave birth to the boy she had always wanted.

- Ruth lost her husband and her identity and went to a strange place that she was not familiar with. But after her season of grief and loneliness, God gave her a wonderful man who took care of her named Boaz.

The process you are currently in might take a while, so don't get in a hurry. We all have goals and dreams that we want to see come to pass even though sometimes we think it is easier to throw in the towel because it's not happening in the timeframe that we think it should be happening in. Stay with God through the process.

Isaiah 40:31 (NLT): "But those who trust in the LORD will find new strength." I challenge you to trust God and to continue the course regardless of the obstacles that come your way because they are going to come whether you want them to or not.

Ephesians 2:10 (Amplified): "For we are God's [own] handiwork (His workmanship), recreated in Christ Jesus, [born anew] that we may do those good works which God predestined (planned beforehand) for us [taking paths which He prepared ahead of time], that we should walk in them [living the good life which He prearranged and made ready for us to live]."

Embracing each experience is not always an easy thing to do, especially the bad and negative ones. But every moment is helping to shape you into the person God wants you to become.

Helen Keller said, "Character cannot be developed in ease and quiet. Only through experiences of trial and suffering can the soul be strengthened, vision cleared, ambition inspired and success achieved." There is purpose in the process that you are in! Your experiences are not in vain. Don't try to go around it or terminate it, but go straight through it and see what will happen. God is molding each of us, and we are all on different pottery wheels in this life. Don't compare yourself to someone whom you think has arrived; focus on the HANDS that are molding you.

"Experience: That most brutal of teachers. But you learn,
my God do you learn."

— C. S. Lewis

WEEK TWENTY-SIX

Sometimes all you can do is just show up.

"No matter how you feel, get up, dress up, and show up for life."
— Regina Brett

You find yourself in a maze, frustrated and perhaps even confused.

You feel disappointment and you may even feel so alone.

You may even feel that sometimes all you have left in you to do is to just show up.

You wonder if it can get any worse,

You're ready to just bail and run,

You find yourself on your knees but have no words that will come out.

You open your Bible, but you have no specific verse that you feel led to read.

You go to church, and everyone has their face plastered on looking the part.

So you go ahead and grab one of your masks and throw it on so you too can look the part.

Everyone seems very spiritual as if they are all up in the heavenly clouds.

But you feel like your feet are burning from the flames of that place called "hell" beneath you.

Then the busybody of the church walks by you and asks how you are doing, but you for sure aren't going to tell her anything.

So you just say, "Doing fine, thanks!"

Then someone comes and lays hands on you and is trying to get you to break through.

You want to tell him to please remove his hands, but you know he would probably get offended or think you are in a bad place.

And maybe you are. Maybe you are just in a different place right now.

Be honest with yourself, and then you can be honest with others.

Find someone safe to talk to.

God already sees your heart; He knows where you are.

You feel nothing; I get that. I've been there before, and I'm sure I'll be there again

So sometimes, yes, it is true that all you have left in you to do is to just show up.

We all feel stuck sometimes in a rut or wrapped up in a struggle that we can't seem to wrestle out of. We all at times feel nothing, and at times we want to ask God, "Why?" about the many things that we experience. But I encourage you to just keep going even when you don't feel like it. Take time to get alone with God, and open your Bible even if the pages never turn, because you never know when God just might speak to you. He speaks to us through the isolated storms that we go through; He speaks to us through those tears that run down our cheeks when nobody is looking. He speaks to us in those simple and still moments of life, He speaks to us through different situations and He can speak to you even when you think it is not the right time, because He is God. He is omnipresent! He knows where you are.

So even if all you have left in you to do is to just show up, do it!

People will change; situations will rock your world and turn you upside down. But there is one thing that remains the same and never changes. Jesus remains the same! Hebrews 13:8: "Jesus Christ is the same yesterday, today, and forever." Whether you're at the bottom ready to give up or on top of the mountain, He still remains the same. He understands your pain, for He took a lot of pain on the cross and it wasn't a quick death. In fact, as He lay dying on the cross with the nails in His hands, His body shifted and He felt it! He felt pure agony! He knows what it's like to feel torn apart! He feels what you are going through as you go through the different seasons in life. He is Jesus, the Prince of Peace, the Beginning and the End. He can guide you through each season in life whether it be good or bad if you will just let Him. He knows right where you are emotionally and spiritually, and He will help you get through this funk and season that you have been in.

So even if all you have left in you to do is to just show up, do it!

Life is not about knowing what is going to happen next because we usually don't have the blueprint available to see it, but you just keep going even when you don't feel like it. Stop waiting for the ideal circumstances to come to make your move.

Psalm 42:11 (Amplified)
"Why are you in despair, O my soul?
Why have you become restless and disquieted within me?
Hope in God and wait expectantly for Him, for I shall yet praise Him, The help of my countenance and my God."

Psalm 118:14: "The LORD is my strength and song,
And He has become my salvation."

WEEK TWENTY-SEVEN

You were born for a purpose

He knew your name before you even knew your own name.
He formed you for a purpose.
You didn't grow nine months in your mother's womb just to exist.

You didn't appear on this earth just by accident.
God didn't just say, "I want to create another female just because."
No, He doesn't do things "just because."
He has a purpose in all that He does,
and you are a part of His purpose.
You were born to fulfill His purpose.

Jeremiah 1:5
"Before I formed you in the womb I knew you;
Before you were born I sanctified you;
I ordained you a prophet to the nations."

As we go through life, there are times we may question our very existence and wonder what we are here for. Sometimes one can think because she were born in an abusive environment or dysfunctional family that she has to stay there. No, you don't! You can rise up and still walk into your purpose, for with God all things are possible!

Romans 8:31: "If God is for us, who can be against us?"

Sometimes life throws us curveballs and sometimes it hands us a crown of thorns, and we wonder what God is doing. It can at times feel as if we are just existing and that no matter what we do we keep hitting a brick wall so we find ourselves on the edge of a cliff. You may have a dream that continues to get pushed to the back burner, maybe life isn't turning out like you thought it would or maybe you are just plain worn out trying.

Maybe you've been burned and it was by someone who is a Christian, so now you've become jaded with church folks and now you are running from the purpose that you know you were called to do. Stop running! Maybe you are one who is starting to question what your purpose is and wondering why God brought you into this world. You may feel frustrated and depressed because you can't seem to get a grasp on what your purpose is.

You were born for a purpose; you were not created to just exist. You were created to bring meaning to your world. You were created to do great things for God. You were created to be light in a dark world and to bring hope to others who feel hopeless. You were created to flourish in your relationships and in life; you were created to see your business grow. You were created to see the church that God has put you over, to exceed your own expectations. You were *formed* by Jesus, the One who died on the cross and who rose again three days later. The One who is the *Great I Am* does all things well and knows right where you are.

I think we all will face the questions sometime in our lives, "What is next?" and "What is my purpose in life?" Stop waiting for the rainbow to come, and go look for it! Step out on faith, pray for guidance and walk into your destiny that He created you for.

What are you passionate about? What dreams have you let go of because you thought you could never achieve them? Are you ignoring His call on your life? Do you think it's too late because you've made some bad decisions? It's never too late to fulfill your calling. You were created to fulfill the calling on your life. He never stops calling; we are the ones who get in the way of our purpose in life. Don't allow anyone to take you away from your calling and purpose, but stay close to God and He will help you fulfill it.

Proverbs 16:9: "A man's heart plans his way,
But the LORD directs his steps."

His plan is much bigger, and you are a part of it. Don't allow your mistakes, setbacks in life, past decisions or people keep you from fulfilling what you were born to do.

You were created for a purpose; find it!

WEEK TWENTY-EIGHT

So long, insecurity

Proverbs 3:26 (Amplified)
"For the Lord will be your confidence, firm and strong,
And will keep your foot from being caught (in a trap)"

We females have to push through our insecurities and let God fulfill the empty closet within that is causing deep-rooted insecurity. If you are looking for affirmation from your relationships alone, then you will continue to live in a cycle. What will you do when the relationship you are in that is thriving and healthy hits a small or a big bump in the road and the person you've leaned on is no longer fulfilling or affirming you? How will you make it then? Relationships go up and down; people will hurt you and disappoint you. But you can remain confident and affirmed if you have a relationship with Christ. He is the same yesterday, today and forever. In fact, the tears we hide and the thoughts we think, He sees them all, so let Him be the One who fulfills you.

What and who fulfills you? When all hell breaks loose in your life if you are rooted in Him He will be the One to affirm you, reassure you and give you the confidence to make the right decisions and help you get through your pain.

After the abuse I experienced about five years later I was still craving certain types of affirmation. I was still insecure and I viewed all men as "that way." I had a bad opinion of myself too. But I met this powerful lady who told me boldly, "Stephenie, you will never

93

be fulfilled or truly feel affirmed until you allow Jesus to be those things in your life that you are looking for in others." That lady was Vani Marshall, a minister and a certified counselor. I got into my prayer closet and started digging into the Word. It changed my outlook on life, people and myself, and it even changed my whole perspective on who Christ was and is in my life. I saw what she was talking about. No matter what people say or do to me, Jesus is my hope and the One who truly affirms me. Yes, I still hurt sometimes (and so will you), and, yes, I don't always understand why some things happen. Yes, I still sometimes cry over things that go deep. But I've also learned that when those feelings of insecurity start rising again I take them to Jesus. I open myself up and hold nothing back. I tell God, "I'm struggling here in a bad way today; I don't understand what is going on around me. Please, help me. O Father, give me confidence and give me peace where I'm struggling. I need You, Jesus." There are times when we will battle insecurities because we are humans filled with imperfections.

We also have the pressure from the glamorous magazines and Hollywood to look a certain way or to be like this and that. We females have to look twenty-one all the time or we are told we are looking old. :-)

I have wrinkles . . . so what!

I'm not as pretty as the lady standing next to me . . . so what!

I don't sing as well as the other lady . . . so what!

I don't have it all together (it seems) as the other lady . . . so what!

I'm slow in trying to get my dream or passion off the ground and everyone is passing me by . . . so what!

Blah, blah, blah . . . so what!

You didn't just enter this world just because. No! He formed you (Psalm 139:13). He took time to put your body parts together, your pretty soft lips in place while forming your hands and feet. You were and still are on His mind.

Don't let others who didn't create you, form you or bring you into this world be the main one to affirm you. Let Jesus affirm you!

Speak this when you are feeling insecure:

He is the I AM (Exodus 3:14).
He is my affirmation.
He is my provider.
He is my calm.
He is my confidence.
He is my healer.

The next time you start feeling insecure, remember that you are not just anybody but you are somebody because you truly are a princess and your Father is the King.

WEEK TWENTY-NINE

Trust Him through your suffering

"Suffering can refine us rather than destroy us because
God himself walks with us in the fire."
— Timothy Keller

I was sound asleep when I heard my phone vibrating on my nightstand.

I was going to ignore it but saw that it was my younger sister, Angela.

It was about 1 AM my time and 11 PM in California.

So I quickly answered and in a sleepy voice I said, "Hello."

Then she began to tell me that something was wrong with Mother.

I heard the fear in her voice and was wishing I was there.

She told me that Mother had a few mini-strokes and was being rushed to the emergency room in an ambulance.

I knew it had to be serious because my mother would never just go into an ambulance unless she was forced to.

So I was up through the night, talking on the phone and texting my siblings.

I was feeling a bit unnerved but at the same time I have to say I felt an inward peace.

After making arrangements I was finally was able to fly out to Stockton and be with my mother for three weeks.

During the time I was there, we had were some scary moments when Mother was not doing too well.

I can tell you that I prayed and quoted Scripture every time an incident outside our control took place.

There were also a few times that I felt like I was back in 2011 when my dad was ill, so that brought on another wave of emotions.

But there was one particular day after we had a rough night trying to get Mother's blood pressure down. (She had never had BP issues before the strokes.) My mother has always been healthy and has never had to go on medication until this happened either.

But since the mini-strokes had happened, her BP was up and down constantly and was causing some other issues.

But this day, I went into her room and we started talking about God. She told me that during the night she was praying and asked God why it was taking so long for her to get better. He gave to her this verse of Scripture: "Blessed is he who is not offended because of Me" (Matthew 11:6).

She told me she cried as He spoke some things to her, and then she said her famous quote, "God does all things well."

I can tell you that moment stuck with me and I took it home with me. I am one who has questioned God with many things and have been frustrated with life not always turning out like I think it should. I am guilty of being one who has complained, and I have had a bad attitude too. I have not done things willingly always, and I have struggled believing. (Just keeping it raw and real with you today.)

I have believed and spoke faith and prayed and even fasted that someone would be healed, and instead he or she died.

I have believed and spoke faith and prayed about a job, a relationship and other serious issues, and they didn't always turn out like I thought they should've turned out so it frustrated me. So I found myself in a struggle believing and asking God why for a while.

Recently I was in a class at church, and my pastor's wife was teaching. She quoted this same passage, Matthew 11:6; "Blessed is he who is not offended because of Me." Then she talked about how John the Baptist was the most powerful and used minister in that day and then he found himself in prison. He was well-known and was used mightily! He questioned God whether or not He was the Son of God, and God sent Matthew 11:6 back to him. I have heard this story all my life and I have told it myself, but in the season I have been in, it really has struck me differently this time.

Not long ago, I humbly went to God and let my walls down and told Him, "Jesus, I give You my plans, my talents, my giftings, all my questions and my will completely. I may not understand what You are doing and where You are taking me, but I surrender everything and trust You no matter what happens in the future." Needless to say, by the time I finished praying I was crying like a baby, but it felt good to release some things that I had been holding back. We all deal with things that nobody even knows we are dealing with because so many of us are good at putting on a facade and just going with the flow. But there are times only God and His grace get us through our suffering. Suffering is hard; it is not something I look forward to. But when we look through the Scriptures we see that many suffered and went through trials and hard times. We also see that many Christians in the Nero days were persecuted and fed to the lions for the cause of Jesus Christ. We will have tribulations, we will struggle and our faith will be tested. Not long ago I was thinking about how the Bible says we will all stand before Him on Judgment Day and will have to answer to Him one on one. I can't lean on my parents or anybody else to get me to heaven; it's between me and God. But as I was thinking about Judgment Day, I was thinking to myself, "What if one of the Christians from the Nero days is one who will be standing by me, who had his limbs ripped apart by a lion and eaten just because he stood for Christ?" I had to think about my life and the things that I complain about and had to ask God to forgive me for my ungratefulness and attitude that takes over sometimes.

Acts 14:22 (Amplified): "strengthening and establishing the hearts of the disciples; encouraging them to remain firm in the faith, saying, 'It is through many tribulations and hardships that we must enter the kingdom of God.' "

Suffering can help us grow in Him. I have found that the more I experience trials and hardships, the more I hunger to go deeper in Christ and have a desire to pray more and to read the Bible more. I am more prone to searching my heart for any clutter that needs to be discarded.

Psalm 26:2: "Examine me, O LORD, and prove me; Try my mind and my heart."

Let the suffering you go through draw you closer to Him.

Let the trials and setbacks in life cause you to pause and look over your life and examine what is going on in the crevices of your heart.

Let the grief push you towards Him so He can wrap you in His arms.

Allow the wounds from the arrows that were meant to destroy you draw you to the Scriptures.

We must realize that no matter what we experience here on earth, whether it be joyful or mourning, pain or happiness, God is preparing us for something that is bigger than you and me. That place is called heaven.

In her book *When God Weeps,* Joni Eareckson Tada writes, "Before my paralysis, my hands reached for a lot of wrong things, and my feet took me into some bad places. After my paralysis, tempting choices were scaled down considerably. My particular affliction is divinely hand-tailored expressly for me. Nobody has to suffer 'transverse spinal lesion at the fourth-fifth cervical' exactly as I did to be conformed to his image.

"God uses suffering to purge sin from our lives, strengthen our commitment to Him, force us to depend on His grace, bind us together with other believers, produce discernment, foster sensitivity, discipline our minds, impart wisdom, stretch our hope, cause us to know Christ better, make us long for truth, lead us to repentance of sin, teach us to give thanks in times of sorrow, increase our faith and strengthen our character. And once He accomplishes such great things, often we can see that our suffering has been worth it."

Every trial that you go through,
Every wound that has you in pain,
Every storm that is rattling your world,
Just know that God is with you through it.
While we have our eyes on the present, He has His eyes on eternity.
May we realize that through each difficulty we go through, God is building our character and preparing us for something greater.
Living here on earth is temporary but heaven is forever. May our hearts be pure, may our motives be right in His sight and may we surrender everything to Him and allow Him to mold us for His purpose for our life.
It's not always comfortable,
It's not always pretty,
It's not always what we want for our lives,
It's not always our personal plan,
But continue to trust His plan.
Cling to Him through each experience and season of suffering in your life.

MONDAY MORNINGS with Stephenie

WEEK THIRTY

Who is your Rock?

Psalm 18:2
"The LORD is my rock and my fortress and my deliverer;
My God, my strength, in whom I will trust;
My shield and the horn of my salvation, my stronghold."

Not long ago, I found myself thinking about the people I view as solid rocks in my life. My mother along with a few others I would consider solid rocks and voices in my life. But my dad immediately came to mind probably because he passed away about five years ago so I think of him often. He was that sound voice in my life; he was that anchor and one who always brought clarity into the situations I was struggling with. So when God decided it was time to take Daddy home, it was very difficult for me to let go of my *rock*. But through this great loss I have turned to Christ in a deeper way. Where Dad was my solid rock and stable voice, Jesus has become much more of that in my life. I have learned that through experiencing trials and hardships we draw closer to Christ, for the bigger picture is heaven.

Matthew 7:24-27 tells us that it is important to build our house on a solid rock and not on shaky ground or sand. When life throws you a curveball or when you find yourself dealing with a situation that is completely out of your control, whom do you turn to? Whom do you lean on through your storms? Your dad, mom, sister, brother, spouse, pastor, counselor or friend? It is always good to have solid people like this in your life but they cannot be your Rock like Jesus can. It is important for us to build a relationship with Christ and to study the Scriptures and know His voice. If you have been on shaky terms with Him and have not been spending much time with Him, you can start today. He longs to hear from you; He will never stop drawing you to Him. While you may have others to whom you turn to help you get through the hard times, don't leave God out. Don't use Him just for emergencies but turn to Him on a daily basis. I think sometimes we forget that the air we breathe is because of Him and that the reason we have a bed to sleep in is because of Him. We must not take Jesus and all of His blessings for granted. He is always a stable and solid voice in our life! We are living in an era where many rocks around us are slippery and unstable, but there is One who will never slip or roll away and leave you alone. His name is Jesus! Cling to the Rock called Jesus, for He will be with you through the ups and downs in life and through the storms that come your way.

I love the lyrics to that old hymn that talks about Christ being our solid Rock. "On Christ the solid Rock I stand; all other ground is sinking sand." I have turned to these lyrics more than once since I lost my rock, my daddy, and have in return started leaning more on Christ for He is a solid Rock. *When everything beneath you is sinking and spiraling, let God be your stability in life. Make sure your foundation is built on a solid rock and not on shallow ground.*

Matthew 7:24-27
Therefore whoever hears these sayings of Mine, and does them, I will liken him to a wise man who built his house on the rock: and the rain descended, the floods came, and the winds blew and beat on that house; and it did not fall, for it was founded on the rock.

But everyone who hears these sayings of Mine, and does not do them, will be like a foolish man who built his house on the sand: and the rain descended, the floods came, and the winds blew and beat on that house; and it fell. And great was its fall.

WEEK THIRTY-ONE

Psalm 23

Psalm 23
The LORD is my shepherd;
I shall not want.
He makes me to lie down in green pastures;
He leads me beside the still waters.
He restores my soul;
He leads me in the paths of righteousness
For His name's sake.
Yea, though I walk through the valley of the shadow of death,
I will fear no evil;
For You are with me;
Your rod and Your staff, they comfort me.
You prepare a table before me in the presence of my enemies;
You anoint my head with oil;
My cup runs over.
Surely goodness and mercy shall follow me
All the days of my life;
And I will dwell in the house of the LORD
Forever.

This psalm is one of the most popular psalms that Christians quote. It brings a calm into our hearts when we are feeling anxious. It reassures us that God is with us no matter what we are facing. It brings peace when we are walking through the unknown. It lets us know that even though we may be wounded, Jesus is the Shepherd and will heal us and deliver us.

I especially gravitate toward verse 4. Here is the Amplified version of it:

"Even though I walk through the [sunless] valley of the shadow of death, I will fear no evil, for You are with me; Your rod [to protect] and Your staff [to guide], they comfort and console me."

When the shepherd would move the sheep from one field to another, they had to go into the valleys to get water from the rivers and streams. There they had to deal with big rocks where wolves, coyotes and wild dogs would hide, ready to attack the sheep. It was dangerous, but that was where the water was. Because the valleys were dangerous, the psalmist called them, "The valley of the shadow of death." The sheep knew their shepherd was with them, and they recognized his voice. He kept them safe from the wild animals and protected them because the wild animals were always hiding, waiting to attack. But the shepherd knew this and kept watch over them.

Whatever type of assignment you are on,

Whatever storm you are in the middle of,

Whatever type of sickness you are battling,

Whatever setback or disappointment you are dealing with,

Whatever relationship issue that has your back against the wall,

Whatever is going on in your home that has you feeling unsettled,

Whatever it is that is keeping you up at night and stressing you out, just know that no matter where you are and where you walk that Jesus is there. His rod will protect you and His staff will guide you.

Matthew 28:20: "Lo, I am with you always."

I have found, having gone through some heartbreaking situations and disappointments, He is indeed with me through them all. I don't always understand what He is doing and where He is taking me, but His rod and His staff guide me and comfort me. Wherever you are on this journey, regardless if you are on a rocky road or maybe everything is going smooth for you right now, just know that whatever the future holds Jesus is with you and will be your comforter through it all.

He is our Shepherd.
He is our Restorer.
He is our Leader.
He is our Guide.
He is our Peace.
Fear no evil, for He is with you,

WEEK THIRTY-TWO

Feeling pressured

E sther had a lot of pressure on her, but she held her own and so can you.

Imagine being a queen over a great nation and having to look the part, keeping up with appearances and having to have every detail down. Little did she know that one of the men (Haman) who had her husband's ear was planning on destroying all the Jews who were in her country. The only problem was that Esther too was a Jew. Esther summoned Hathach, one of the king's eunuchs whom the king had appointed to attend her, to speak to her uncle Mordecai to find out what was going on, for he was acting strange, morbid and sad. After Hathach returned, he told her the news about Haman's plan to destroy the Jews. Esther was feeling distressed, rattled and fearful for her people and for herself. She told Hathach to tell her uncle to have all the Jews fast three days and three nights with her, she and her maids would also fast and then she would approach the king to tell him about Haman's plans. Esther 4:16 (Amplified) always speaks to me. "Then I will go in to [see] the king [without being summoned], which is against the law; and if I perish, I perish." Esther did what was right even under great pressure and saved her people from being destroyed. Haman, who had plotted to kill Mordecai on the gallows, was taken there himself, and the king ordered him to be hung there.

What kind of pressure are you under today? What decision are you being faced with today? What are you stressed about today?

Have you prayed about it? Have you fasted about it? Our decisions can affect us for a lifetime or can at least take us on a long detour before we get back on the right track.

In the past I have found for myself that when I feel pressure about something and feel stressed about it, I need to stop and pray about it. If we are not careful we will make the wrong decision because of the pressure we feel from others. So if you are feeling pressured, please don't just make a rash decision to get someone off your back or to be a part of something that you have been wanting to be a part of for a long time because you want to fit in. If you have to compromise who you are to fit in, then run from it. If it is not the right thing to do, don't do it! Don't give in to pressure!

Proverbs 24:10: "If you faint in the day of adversity,
Your strength is small."

The Message version reads like this: "If you fall to pieces in a crisis, there wasn't much to you in the first place." That is pretty blunt and to the point. I am glad that Esther stood strong in the face of adversity.

She could've easily ignored the pleas of her uncle and others. She could've cared more about her position, the popularity, being on a big stage and enjoying the attention she was getting because of her status in life. But somewhere deep inside, she had some roots that she never got away from. It rose within her, and the compassion and passion for her tribe and people became greater than the glitter and tangible things that surrounded her. Let her story motivate you to make the right decisions while under pressure. I pray that Esther will be a role model for all of us women to look to when we feel like we have to give in because we don't want to stand out or be ridiculed for our values and our faith in Jesus Christ.

Wherever you are in life right now, you can make it! You can make the right decision! I challenge you to take this week to earnestly pray, and if you are able, fast about the decisions that you are needing to make. Your decisions become who you are. Your decisions not only affect you but affect your children, your close relationships and your destiny.

Esther 5:1-2: "On the third day [of the fast] . . . Esther put on her royal robes and stood in the inner court of the king's palace, across from the king's house, while the king sat on his royal throne in the royal house, facing the main entrance of the house. So it was, when the king saw Queen Esther standing in the court, that she found favor in his sight, and the king held out to Esther the golden scepter that was in his hand. Then Esther went near and touched the top of the scepter."

MONDAY MORNINGS *with* Stephenie

WEEK THIRTY-THREE

Sometimes it's your battle to fight

There will be times when you will walk through the valley alone (without your inner circle, friends and posse) because it's your battle, your process and your calling.

In Genesis 37 we read the story of Joseph. He had a lot of dreams when he was a young boy about how he was going to rule and be used in a powerful way. We also see that his brothers didn't like it too much being told their little brother would be ruler over them. I guess most of us wouldn't be too happy hearing someone tell us that he is going to be ruler over us and we are going to bow to him. So the brothers got a plan together to get rid of this younger brother who was pestering them and who was their father's favorite. In Genesis 27:23-24, "So it came to pass, when Joseph had come to his brothers, that they stripped Joseph of his tunic, the tunic of many colors that was on him. Then they took him and cast him into a pit. And the pit was empty; there was no water in it."

This was all a part of Joseph's personal journey. I don't know why he had to go into a pit, be sold into slavery and had to deal with his boss's wife trying to seduce him, but Joseph said, "No way!" because he cared more about what God thought about him than what anybody else thought about him. (He wanted to please God.) So she lied about him and had him thrown into prison. But while he lay in prison, God gave him the interpretation of dreams. (Imagine that, Joseph in a dark place but still being used by God.) He eventually found favor with Pharaoh and was called to interpret one of his dreams that had been troubling him. Joseph had remained humble even when he was rejected by his own family; even when he was lied about and was thrown in prison, he still stayed the course. God was watching him through the circumstances that Joseph found himself in. Joseph didn't have a support group, friends or family to cheer him on or to encourage him. He was in it alone. Then the time came when God elevated Joseph to be a ruler in the land of Egypt. God's favor doesn't always come when we expect it but it usually comes after we have gone through some trials and have walked the valley alone.

Genesis 41:39-45

Then Pharaoh said to Joseph, "Inasmuch as God has shown you all this, there is no one as discerning and wise as you. You shall be over my house, and all my people shall be ruled according to your word; only in regard to the throne will I be greater than you." And Pharaoh said to Joseph, "See, I have set you over all the land of Egypt."
Then Pharaoh took his signet ring off his hand and put it on Joseph's hand; and he clothed him in garments of fine linen and put a gold chain around his neck. And he had him ride in the second chariot which he had; and they cried out before him, "Bow the knee!" So he set him over all the land of Egypt. Pharaoh also said to Joseph, "I am Pharaoh, and without your consent no man may lift his hand or foot in all the land of Egypt." And Pharaoh called Joseph's name Zaphnath-Paaneah. And he gave him as a wife Asenath, the daughter of Poti-Pherah priest of On. So Joseph went out over all the land of Egypt.

God will come through for you! He raised Joseph up and used him in spite of what others did to him. He saw something in Joseph that let Him know He could trust Joseph. God put Joseph in a position that not even his brothers could take away from him because it was God who put him there. Joseph remained faithful to God until he died. So if you feel you are in the battle alone, just know that God is with you through it.

Don't give up while you are in the battle.

Don't give in while you are in the process.

Don't throw in the towel while you are in the valley.

This is temporary and not a permanent season.

The prison you are in isn't forever.

The pit of discouragement and depression you find yourself in is temporary.

Allow Him to develop in you His character while you are walking alone in this season. Remain faithful to God, and He will bring you out and take you to places you thought weren't possible.

WEEK THIRTY-FOUR

Don't put God in a box

Isaiah 55:8-9: "For My thoughts are not your thoughts,
Nor are your ways My ways," says the LORD.
"For as the heavens are higher than the earth,
So are My ways higher than your ways,
And My thoughts than your thoughts."

This scripture is easy to quote but can be difficult to live when trying to understand God's ways. When you read the story of Joshua and how he led the people of Israel to conquer the city of Jericho, it may cause you to scratch your head and wonder how it could've actually happened that way for it doesn't make sense how it all unraveled. Joshua and his men scoped out Jericho first and went into the city as spies and then came back to their camp, and from there the Lord instructed them to march around the city of Jericho once a day for six days and seven times the seventh day and then told them that the city would crumble. It sounds like a movie and a little farfetched to the human mind. But nevertheless it happened! It is time for women to get into sync with God's plan, realize that His ways are not our ways and stop putting Him in the box that we think He should be in. It doesn't matter what we think about a situation or how we think He should do it because God is going to do it in His own way and in His own time.

Joshua 6:1-5 (Amplified)
Now Jericho [a fortified city with high walls] was tightly
closed because [of the people's fear] of the sons of Israel;
no one went out or came in. The Lord said to Joshua, "See,
I have given Jericho into your hand, with its king and the
mighty warriors. Now you shall march around the city, all
the men of war circling the city once. You shall do this [once
each day] for six days. Also, seven priests shall carry seven
trumpets [made] of rams' horns ahead of the ark; then on
the seventh day you shall march around the city seven times,
and the priests shall blow the trumpets. When they make a
long blast with the ram's horn, and when you hear the
sound of the trumpet, all the people shall cry out with a
great shout (battle cry); and the wall of the city will fall down
in its place, and the people shall go up, each man [going]
straight ahead [climbing over the rubble]."

Some things God does are just way over our heads, and we will
never figure it out because He does things in His own way. Romans
11:33: "Oh, the depth of the riches both of the wisdom and
knowledge of God! How unsearchable are His judgments and His
ways past finding out!"

Are you praying for something that you desperately need
from Him?

Is your body wracked with pain?

Is your child making wrong decisions and no longer serving God?

Is your spouse cold towards you or perhaps he has walked out
on you and you are now alone?

Are you restless and ready for change?

What do you need from Him today?

Keep in mind while you pray and while you wait that He may not come through the front door like you are expecting Him to.

He may instead come through the window or through the roof.

Be open to His ways even when it doesn't make sense for Jesus operates in a realm that the human mind cannot grasp because the natural eye cannot see the supernatural. The definition of supernatural is: "a manifestation or event) attributed to some force beyond scientific understanding or the laws of nature." Tap into His ways and watch what happens. Pray and believe that He is working it out and that He is doing something even when you see nothing happening. He will come through, but it will be in His own time and on His own terms. We serve a God who does things that are unconventional and not the norm, so open the box, let your faith run freely and believe that God is working on your behalf. Open the box, spread your wings and let faith and God take you to a higher place that will plug you into the supernatural, a place where God moves freely and can do for you what no other person can do for you. This is a place where He does the impossible, a place where He heals, a place where He restores someone whom everyone has given up on, a place where He makes your dreams a reality, a place where He births within you a new season and takes you to a new level in Him. Step out of the box and go for it!

MONDAY MORNINGS *with Stephenie*

WEEK THIRTY-FIVE

Take time for yourself

Matthew 11:28: "Come to Me, all you who labor and
are heavy laden, and I will give you rest."

A re you one who is constantly giving to others but you barely take time to take care of yourself?

Is your home sometimes a war zone and in an uproar and you want desperately just to escape?

Are you tired of doing everything and being the glue in your relationships, and now the glue is starting to melt and you are about to have a meltdown?

Have you been carrying the load for a long time, and it's starting to take its toll on you?

I talk to women from all walks who sometimes feel tired and feel they can't go on much longer. They are trying to hold it together but inside are crumbling and falling apart. Whether it is from stress in a marriage, with a child, a job, a ministry or just life, they feel they are at their wit's end.

Many females will tell you they don't have time to take a break; they are too busy. Yes, we are all very busy and trying to hold it together. But it is imperative that you take time out for yourself sometimes. It's impossible to give to others what you don't have. I say often, "You can't give what you don't have." If you don't have it in you, the lack will eventually be revealed and can bring sickness, extra mental stress, relationship issues and unwanted emotional issues and can cause you to put a wall up and shut out those you love. Please take time for yourself.

"Self-care is never selfish,
but it may feel that way when you live a frenzied life."
— Arthur P. Ciaramicoli

Things you can do:
• Get a pedicure,

• a facial,

• a massage;

• go to a cafe and buy a coffee and read a book;

• make a day for antique shopping;

• do something you've been wanting to do (for you).

If you are low on funds, you can create your own spa at home:
Light a candle.

Make a hot cup of coffee, hot tea and allow yourself to have a dessert with it (just this once). If you are like me, eat something chocolate; I am a chocoholic.

Take a hot bath and put some bath salts and essential oils in there and relax your mind.

Tell your family that you are going into your bedroom and need an hour or two by yourself to relax your mind and do what you want to do.

Allow yourself to feel.

Write out a plan and make a list of goals.

Write out the dream that you have pushed to the back burner.

Pray, meditate and find a verse of Scripture that will uplift you and encourage you.

Try to schedule some alone time like this on a weekly basis. (We all need alone time to refuel.)

Jesus Himself also took time away from the crowd.

Luke 5:16 (Amplified): "Jesus Himself would often slip away to the wilderness and pray [in seclusion]."

If you don't take care of yourself and protect your emotions and heart when necessary, no one else will. After you die, you will be replaced. I don't mean to sound insensitive, but it is true. Yes, people will cry and miss you and say nice things about you, but eventually you will be just another memory for others to talk about. So take care of you because no one else will do it for you. Acts 1:8 reminds us that it is important that we be good witnesses for other people. Taking care of your personal needs (emotionally) will help you be a good witness to the world. First Corinthians 6:19: "Do you not know that your body is the temple of the Holy Spirit who is in you, whom you have from God, and you are not your own?" You can take care of your temple by taking time out for yourself and recharging and refueling your mind.

What have you been wanting to do for a long time but keep putting it off because you keep putting everyone and everything else above your needs, telling yourself that one day you will do it? Why not do it now? You matter too, and you matter to God! If you don't take care of your own needs, you will find yourself in a vulnerable place struggling emotionally and maybe even spiritually. So today make plans to do something for yourself this week.

MONDAY MORNINGS with Stephenie

WEEK THIRTY-SIX

Don't become a chronic condition

Isaiah 43:18-19
Do not remember the former things,
Nor consider the things of old.
Behold, I will do a new thing,
Now it shall spring forth;
Shall you not know it?
I will even make a road in the wilderness
And rivers in the desert

I journal often and found this from 2015 and thought it so appropriate for our current culture.

Don't allow damaged emotions to become your chronic condition.

Don't allow guilt from the past to become your chronic condition.

Don't allow fear of rejection to become your chronic condition.

Don't allow the anger that you are suppressing to become your chronic condition.

Don't allow open wounds to become your chronic condition.

Don't allow unforgiveness to become your chronic condition.

Don't allow insecurity to become your chronic condition.

Don't allow the facade you wear to become your chronic condition.

Don't allow the fear to love again to become your chronic condition.

Don't allow someone's negative opinion of you to become your chronic condition.

Don't allow the abuse that you endured for years and years to become your chronic condition.

Don't allow a setback in life to become your chronic condition.

Don't allow a betrayal by someone you loved and trusted to become your chronic condition.

Don't allow the fear to move forward to become your chronic condition.

Don't allow Satan to continue playing in the playground that he has built inside your mind to become your chronic condition.

Why go another year, another day and another hour?

Face it today! Seek Christian professional counseling if necessary with someone who is in tune with Christ and take authority over the emotions and wounds that have controlled you thus far. Allow Jesus to get inside of the "thing" that has been controlling you for too long. Don't let it become your chronic condition and don't allow yourself to become immune to it. It's time to take control of your life today and to do something about it! It's time to call it for what it is! It's time to look it straight in the face and tell it to leave once and for all! Let Jesus heal you; let Him restore your mind and take away years of pain that you've been holding on to.

We are lost without Him. . . . We can only be complete with Him.

I like how the Message version breaks down Isaiah 43:18-19.
"Forget about what's happened;
don't keep going over old history.
Be alert, be present. I'm about to do something brand-new.
It's bursting out! Don't you see it?
There it is! I'm making a road through the desert,
rivers in the badlands."

Having been someone who has experienced abuse, I can tell you that the emotions you deal with after you are out of it can be the most challenging part. If you are not careful, your emotions, the baggage that you carry and the victim mentality can become a chronic condition. An emotional chronic condition is a place where you become comfortable living in that mind-set. I had to push myself out of this mind-set because I realized that it was becoming a chronic condition in my heart. I continued to blame the person who had hurt me but I was doing nothing about it. I was licking my wounds and giving myself a pity party. After all, I was the victim here! But I came to a place where I had to ask myself, "What are you going to do about it? Are you going to stay there and continue justifying your attitude and refusal to change yourself?" But I finally looked myself in the mirror and faced it! It was not easy though, and even after I decided I was changing, I still would sometimes struggle internally wanting to stay where I was. You see, it can become comfortable living there; also, if your circle of friends are coddling you, feeding your dysfunction and the victim mentality that you have, you take the risk of staying tied to your emotional chronic condition longer.

I ask you today, "Whom are you listening to?" and "What are you going to do to change your circumstances?" How are you going to change how your story will end? Don't put down the pen but instead turn the page, keep writing and stop letting a chronic condition be your compass in life.

So you've been rejected and hurt; are you going to stay there and wallow in it and stay the same? You have a choice to either break out of it or you can stay there and become more and more miserable. We all have a choice! The truth hurts sometimes. I remember when I was living in Washington, DC, and was dating a guy who told me that I had issues and that I needed to get help. I got angry with him and tried to deny it, but I knew in my heart that although I had moved on from the abuse physically, I was still living there emotionally. I had to do something about it because it was affecting my relationships. When something unhealthy is consuming you, you cannot focus on doing something positive because positive versus negativity don't mix well. It's one or the other; which path do you choose to take today?

"Incredible change happens in your life when you decide to take control of what you do have power over instead of craving control over what you don't."
— Steve Maraboli,

You can do it! There are many who have been through a lot of pain and unfortunate circumstances, but they have risen above it! I challenge you to face the chronic conditions that have made their way into your heart and to change them. You can do whatever you set your mind to do, but you have to want to change. That is the key to freedom. You have to want it bad enough to change your ways and your thoughts. You have to discard the cloak of apathy, stop with the excuses, face yourself in the mirror and change. Where do you want to be a year from today? If you don't change, you will be here a year from now making up the same excuses. Start today, for you can do it!

Ephesians 4:22-24 (Amplified)
That, regarding your previous way of life, you put off your old self [completely discard your former nature], which is being corrupted through deceitful desires, and be continually renewed in the spirit of your mind [having a fresh, untarnished mental and spiritual attitude], and put on the new self [the regenerated and renewed nature], created in God's image, [godlike] in the righteousness and holiness of the truth [living in a way that expresses to God your gratitude for your salvation].

WEEK THIRTY-SEVEN

Soar above the noise

"But those who hope in the Lord will renew their strength. They will soar on wings like eagles; they will run and not grow weary, they will walk and not be faint" Isaiah 40:31 (NIV).

I've heard my parents say this many times while I grew up, "You can't soar like an eagle while hanging out with the chickens."

So what does that mean? Basically, eagles don't get involved in petty things such as drama, gossip, negativity and other things that could bring them down. But chickens, unlike eagles, like to peck a lot, fight and never seem content. Chickens are bound to this earth while eagles have a vision to fly above the earth and the noise. Life already is hectic enough, so why surround yourself with voices that have a chicken mentality and that will peck the life out of you? You may be struggling with depression, anxiety, insecurity and many of the other things that we (women) sometimes battle. So why let those who have a chicken mentality hang out with you and feed you their negative opinions? What you need to do is to say good-bye to the chicken mentality and find some eagles to fly with. Eagles aren't going to let you bring negativity into their group; they have fought long and hard to get where they are and have been vigilant in keeping above the noise. It's time to change your thinking so you can also fly and soar like an eagle.

We must rely on God to get us through the rough patches in life.

Ephesians 6:10: "Be strong in the Lord and in the power of His might."

You might not feel strong enough to break away from the dysfunction or the unhealthy situation that you are in, but with God you can. Let Jesus be your wings! Let Him help you fly above the noise that has been consuming your mind and taking over your thoughts. In order to truly soar like an eagle, you have to let go of what is keeping you tied to the chicken mentality mind-set. You can do all things through Christ which strengthens you as Philippians 4:13 tells us, but you have to believe it for yourself.

The eagle mentality sees a way out.

The chicken mentality sees what is in front of him.

The eagle mentality wants to fly and to be what God has created him to be.

The chicken mentality wants to stay in his comfort zone.

The eagle mentality doesn't let the circumstances keep him down.

The chicken mentality focuses on the circumstances and can't break out of the chicken coop.

The eagle is going to rise above and go high, away from the chicken mentality . . . and so can you!

"They are angry with me, because I know what I am," said the little eagle. "How do you know that they are angry with you?" "Because they despise me for wanting to soar; they only want me to peck at the dirt, looking for ants with them. But I can't do that. I don't have chicken feet; I have eagle wings." "And what is so wrong with having eagle wings and no chicken feet?" asked the old owl. "I'm not sure; that's what I'm trying to find out." "They hate you because you know that you are an eagle and they want you to think you are a chicken so that you will peck at the ground

looking for ants and worms, so that you will never know that you are an eagle and always think yourself a chicken. Let them hate you. They will always be chickens, and you will always be an eagle. You must fly. You must soar."
said the old owl.

— C. JoyBell C.

MONDAY MORNINGS with Stephenie

WEEK THIRTY-EIGHT

Get out of the boat

Matthew 14:28-29, Amplified
"Peter replied to Him, "Lord, if it is [really] You, command me to come to You on the water." He said, "Come!" So Peter got out of the boat, and walked on the water and came toward Jesus."

Every time I read the story about Peter, it always inspires me to reach for things that look impossible. I have heard some ridicule Peter for his lack of faith, but I actually admire him for at least having enough courage to step out of the boat. In verse 30 Peter began to realize that he was walking on water and took his eyes off Jesus and then began to slip and sink. In Matthew 14 we are told the disciples were all on a boat and found themselves in the middle of a storm. The boat began rocking back and forth and they all became afraid, but then they saw a figure walking on the water and thought it was a ghost. Then in verse 27 Jesus said, "Take courage, it is I! Be not afraid!" That is when Peter became bold and courageous and then pushed himself out of the boat and into the water. He began to walk towards Jesus, but somewhere along the way he got his eyes on the water instead of the One who was walking on water, and began to sink. But he still had the faith to get out of the boat and walk towards Jesus.

Many people play it safe like the disciples in the boat who were afraid to step out and take a risk. But I challenge you to take a risk with Christ. What has He been asking you to do? What has He called you to do but you have been ignoring it? What have you been feeling you need to do with your life but you have been afraid to step out of the boat and just go for it? I too struggle with this sometimes. When I get my eyes on the water, that's when I start looking at the what if's and comparing myself with other people. I then find myself going back into the boat and playing it safe. But when I spend time with God and dig into His Word, I get bold and I am confident that I can do it! There is something about believing in a power that is bigger than your own. There is something about believing in a supernatural power that can make a broken person whole and heal a body that is full of a terminal disease. There is something about believing in a higher power that can change the hearts of man. His name is Jesus!

Get out of the boat called Fear.
Get out of the boat called Apathy.
Get out of the boat called Insecurity.
Get out of the boat called "Comparing yourself with others" and just do something about it! Get some fire in your belly!
What is His voice telling you to do?
What have you been ignoring?
What have you pushed to the back burner?
It's time to step out of the boat, and it's time to walk on water!

1. Don't allow distractions to keep you from leaving the boat.

2. Get rid of the doubt that is trying to defeat your purpose.

3. Your faith will be tested by those who stay in the boat.

4. If you're going to walk on water you will have to get out of the boat (your comfort zone).

Remember, when you step out to walk on the water with Him, He will be with you every step of the way. He will never leave us nor forsake us according to Hebrews 13:5.

WEEK THIRTY-NINE

Do you have enough oil for your journey?

Matthew 25:1-13 (Amplified)

Then the kingdom of heaven will be like ten virgins, who took their lamps and went to meet the bridegroom. Five of them were foolish [thoughtless, silly, and careless], and five were wise [far-sighted, practical, and sensible]. For when the foolish took their lamps, they did not take any [extra] oil with them, but the wise took flasks of oil along with their lamps. Now while the bridegroom was delayed, they all began to nod off, and they fell asleep. But at midnight there was a shout, "Look! The bridegroom [is coming]! Go out to meet him." Then all those virgins got up and put their own lamps in order [trimmed the wicks and added oil and lit them]. But the foolish virgins said to the wise, "Give us some of your oil, because our lamps are going out." But the wise replied, "No, otherwise there will not be enough for us and for you, too; go instead to the dealers and buy oil for yourselves." But while they were going away to buy oil, the bridegroom came, and those who were ready went in with him to the wedding feast; and the door was shut and locked. Later the others also came, and said, "Lord, Lord, open [the door] for us." But He replied, "I assure you and most solemnly say to you, I do not know you [we have no relationship]."Therefore, be on the alert [be prepared and ready], for you do not know the day nor the hour [when the Son of Man will come].

The ten virgins all started with their lamps full of oil. They were all headed to the same place. They were all prepared and ready to meet the bridegroom. They were all excited to see Him. But somewhere along the way, five of those virgins allowed something to get in the way and it kept them from seeing the bridegroom.

"Do you have enough oil for your journey?" "Are you full of Him?"

What are some of the things that deplete us, distract us and keep us from focusing on the oil in our lamps? What was it for them?

Here are some things that we struggle with, that cause us to get our focus off what is important:

- unforgiveness

- lying

- offenses

- bitterness

- addictions

- pornography

- unhealthy relationships

- infidelity

- apathy for the things of God

- giving into temptations

- listening to the wrong voices

- distractions

- selfishness

- jealousy

- justifying our sins

All of the ten virgins were a part of the church. They went to church and maybe some even sang on the praise team, greeted on Sundays, played an instrument, preached a sermon, organized meals for those who had a family member pass away and did good deeds for others. These are all great things to do for the kingdom of God, but being faithful isn't being fruitful and being faithful isn't what is going to secure you a place in the bridegroom party. Matthew 25 is very clear about this. We must not think that our good deeds alone will keep our lamps full because they will not.

This past year I have felt a sense of urgency and have found myself feeling the urge to pray more for my family, my friends and my soul. We are surrounded by so much brokenness, dysfunction, narcissism, unforgiveness, hatred, jealousy, bitterness and pride, but we the church have the answer! But if our attitude is like the world, we are hurting the gospel of Jesus Christ! How can our lamps be full when we mimic the world and when we are just as hateful as the world? Don't use social media to spew hateful rhetoric but give someone hope, for we are living in a world that is dying and we are *all* just a breath away from eternity. John 10:10 tells us that Satan is out to steal, kill and destroy. He will use people to try to destroy you and take you down the wrong path too, so be alert and aware of your surroundings. Try the voices in your life! Protect your heart and your home at all costs. Protect the oil that is in your lamp.

We women need to get on our knees and pray. In fact, before you go on social media, before you go to work and before you start your day, pray like David prayed, "Create in me a clean heart, Lord. Help me to run from danger, help me to bow out gracefully from drama and help me, Lord, to show You through my words and actions." We need to be full of prayer and the Word. It is impossible to have enough oil on this journey if we are never spending time with Him. He is the One who fills our lamps with oil. Let Him help you overcome your temptations and the things that are trying to steal your oil. You can't live on yesterday's oil.

What is missing in your lamp?

How much oil do you have in your lamp?

Do you have enough oil to get you through the fire and through the storm, or will you cave because you are not full of Him?

What do you need to change in your life that is getting in the way of your lamp's being full of Him?

May we all search our hearts and check our lamps and make sure our lamps are full for the journey.

Matthew 25:2-4 (NIV)

"Five of them were foolish and five were wise. The foolish ones took their lamps but did not take any oil with them. The wise, however, took oil in jars along with their lamps."

WEEK FORTY

You can't (always) fix it

"Perhaps what you are trying to fix God is trying to break." Ouch!

I know that is hard to grasp, but we females sometimes do try to hold things together while the whole time God is trying to fix it in His own way.

After I had experienced abuse and heartache, I became very jaded with religion, church and Christianity and went from a worship leader to a prodigal running from it all. My mother wanted to put my heart back together and fix me, but she could not fix me. There I was a young adult trying to find my way, and on several occasions my mother would step in to try to save me from making a mistake. She would do her best to advise me on different situations I was dealing with. I knew she didn't want me to mess up my life, but I was one of those stubborn individuals who was going to have to experience it for myself in order to truly learn, kind of like the old Frank Sinatra song, "I did it my way." Therefore I did choose my own path, and, yes, I did fall not just once but I fell many times flat on my face. I have tasted the bitter wind and have felt the sting of pain hit me straight in the face. I have cried a bucketful of tears, and not all of it was because of bad choices I had made. Sometimes just plain ol' life can wreak havoc on you and cause you to become fragile, hardened and wounded. My mother could not fix me. She could not take the stubbornness out of me or force me to make the right choices in life, but I had to learn for myself. As I journeyed through the difficult pathways in my life, she and my father continued to pray for me; they loved me through my pain and were always there for me regardless where I was in life. My parents had to sit back and watch God mold me into what He wanted me to be. Today I am thankful for the love they have always shown me. Through the many storms I have been in, some have seemed gigantic and I wondered if I would get through them. But here I am; I survived it. As I have gone through the different treacherous tests in life, I have come to the conclusion that I would rather be in the arms of Christ while going through a storm than to be far away, trying to navigate through life without Him to lean on and cling to. Please do yourself a favor, and grasp the understanding that you sometimes will not be able to fix the other person. There may come a time when you will need to let go and allow someone to learn from the choices that he or she makes in his or her own life. Allow God to walk with you as you learn to let go and stop trying to fix things that are out of your control.

First Peter 5:7 (Amplified): "Casting the whole of your care [all your anxieties, all your worries, all your concerns, once and for all] on Him, for He cares for you affectionately and cares about you watchfully."

Some of my experiences changed my life. My parents couldn't save me, but it took God allowing me to go through some things to get my attention. If you are concerned about ones close to your heart who are making the wrong decisions and who are going in the wrong direction, give them to Jesus. You can love them through it, but it is important for you to let go completely of the reins and allow Jesus to take over the situation that you have been stressing yourself out over. He loves them more than you, and He knows right where they are. So stop trying to fix something that God is trying to break (fix).

Never stop praying for them.
Never stop fasting for them.
Never stop speaking life over them.
See them coming back. . . . Speak it!
He will bring them back home and will put them back together.

WEEK FORTY-ONE

Are you sick and tired of being sick and tired?

Luke 8:46-48 (KJV)

And Jesus said, Somebody hath touched me: for I perceive that virtue is gone out of me. And when the woman saw that she was not hid, she came trembling, and falling down before him, she declared unto him before all the people for what cause she had touched him, and how she was healed immediately. And he said unto her, Daughter, be of good comfort: thy faith hath made thee whole; go in peace.

For twelve long years she dealt with this sickness, and then one day she became sick and tired of being sick and tired.

What was it on that particular day that caused her to push her way through a large crowd to where Jesus was and to touch the hem of His garment? It seems to me that if she were touching the hem of His garment that she was sitting pretty low to the ground. Could it be that she was in so much pain that she was having to crawl her way to Jesus? Could it be that she was so weak in her body that she could barely get to Him? There was something in this broken woman that inspires me because in spite of her sickness she refused to stay there and curl up in a fetal position and die.

In spite of her circumstances,

In spite of the curveballs that were being thrown at her,

In spite of her sickness,

She found a way out!

We don't hear anything about her family, but could it be that they had given up on her? After all, it had been twelve long years she had been sick, so perhaps they just came to terms that she would be this way for the rest of her life. I mean, let's face it, how many people do we know who have been dealing with a disease or something for a very long time and we've acclimated to it? "It's just the way it is," some may say. But in Luke 8:48 Jesus told her, "Your faith has made you whole."

Could it be that Jesus is waiting on you to walk towards Him even if you have to crawl your way to touch the hem of His garment? How desperate are you for your healing? Are you struggling with your emotions that have become fragile from a past situation? How much do you want to hear from Him? Is He waiting on you to take a step of faith? Is He waiting on you to do something about your dilemma?

She went to Him; He didn't go to her. She forced herself out so that she could receive her healing.

Do you need to push yourself out?

Do you need to force yourself out?

Do you need to stop saying, "It is what it is"?

Do you need to stop saying, "I've been this way for twelve years and nothing is changing"?

Rise up! Do something about the situation you are in!

Start walking towards Him. Speak faith and speak life into your situation! Be persistent. Continue to climb the mountain even if you have to take a few breaks, but don't stop completely. You can do it!

Proverbs 18:21: "Death and life are in the power of the tongue,
And those who love it will eat its fruit."

WEEK FORTY-TWO

Speak faith into your situation

II Corinthians 5:7: "For we walk by faith, not by sight."

When I was a teenager I remember a particular time that my mom had a growth that grew to the size of a lemon under her chin. She went to see the doctor about it, and he wanted to do extensive testing on it and have it removed. But I remember as if it were yesterday that mom began to thank God for removing it. She began to fast and pray, and daily my siblings and I would hear her say, "It's gone in Jesus' name!" And "I command you, growth, to dry up and go back to hell where you belong!" She just believed it. While it may sound crazy to some, it is the reality of who my mother is. She just believes and speaks it into existence. She has spent her entire life consumed with the things of God. Prayer, fasting, and the Word are her staples in life. So as crazy as it may sound to some, about six months later I saw this growth completely disappear. Yes, you heard right! It miraculously disappeared! Her doctor was so astounded by it that he put in her file that it just disappeared. Yes, crazy faith Mom has always had. You can't argue with something supernatural.

I asked my mom not long ago, what was going through her mind when she would woke up every morning and saw the growth still there. I asked her how she kept the faith and believed that God would heal her. This is her response. "I truly believed Mark 11:22-23 and stood firm on that Word Jesus spoke." Then she quoted to me Mark 9:29 (KJV): "This kind goeth not out but by prayer and fasting."

Believe in the impossible and believe that God is working on your behalf.

I have struggled with faith and believing in the impossible. Some things have challenged my faith and have caused me to have to dig deeper into the Word. I've had to pray and ask Jesus to increase my faith and to decrease my negative thinking. I have seen God do some incredible things and miracles, yet there are still times I have trouble believing in something that I cannot see physically. But I have learned that in order to believe you have to be plugged into prayer and into something that is beyond human reasoning because that is who Christ is. He operates in a realm that we cannot grasp and see with just our human intellect. Oftentimes we struggle with believing and having faith because we have been bombarded by life. Distractions have gotten in the way, and sadly, even people in our inner circle can bring a negative vibe into our mind-set if we allow them to. Romans 8:6: "For to be carnally minded is death, but to be spiritually minded is life and peace." I cannot stress enough how important it is to guard your mind from things that are pulling at your faith and belief system. Protect your faith! Protect your belief system! Protect your mind!

You may say, "But God didn't heal one of my family members or my best friend, so how can I believe?" I understand that question for I have asked it myself. But even when God decides to take someone we love home to be with Him, He never stops doing miracles, healing and restoring people here on earth. My faith is in Him and in His plan. We must trust Him and believe that He does all things well. God loves us and He has a plan, but that doesn't mean life is always going to be easy. We are going to go through difficult seasons, and things will happen that do not seem fair.

John 16:33 (Amplified): "I have told you these things, so that in Me you may have [perfect] peace. In the world you have tribulation and distress and suffering, but be courageous [be confident, be undaunted, be filled with joy]; I have overcome the world."

It's so important for us to understand this so we won't be confused and lose our faith in Him when life gets hard. In spite of what we feel sometimes, we cannot sit idle and go down without a fight. Today I challenge you to ignite yourself with some fire and passion and start believing in something that you cannot see and start believing in something that is bigger than yourself. I've seen enough to know that we serve a God who does mighty things and who answers prayer.

Deuteronomy 10:21: "He is your praise, and He is your God, who has done for you these great and awesome things which your eyes have seen."

Even when you don't feel it,
Even when you don't feel like doing it,
Do it anyway!
We can't walk by what we feel and by what we see. If we do, we will never get from plan A to plan B. Jesus works in the realm of the impossible, so believe even when you see nothing happening. Speak faith into your situation!

WEEK FORTY-THREE

Know who you are . . . in Christ

In Matthew 16:13 Jesus asked His disciples, "Who do men say
that I . . . am?" The disciples responded in verse 14: "So they
said, 'Some say John the Baptist, some Elijah, and others
Jeremiah or one of the prophets.' " Then in verse 15 Jesus said
again, "But who do you say that I am?" Simon famously replied,
"You are the Christ, the Son of the living God."

D o you know who you are in Christ? Sadly, we often look
around and see Christian women who are wounded and
tucking their heads, looking defeated and insecure. I used
to be that way. I used to have that mind-set because I had allowed
unhealthy things to grow inside my heart and allowed voices to
make me feel worthless. The problem isn't coming from what they
believe about you; it's coming from what you believe about
yourself. Who are you? Step onto your purpose, God's purpose!
Don't let just anybody define you . . . mold you . . . control you . . .
make you. They didn't create you, so stop giving them power!

Don't let your past become your identity.

Don't let your mistakes define who you are.

You are more than that!

We live in a culture where we are too concerned with what
people think about us. Some will hold your past over your head, and
that in itself can cause you to want to hide in a corner and not do
anything for God. But what does God think about you? He is the One

who brought you into this world, He is the One who called you, He is the One who created you but it seems at times we are more concerned with what our peers think about us. Stop allowing the pressures in this world to dictate to you how you should feel about yourself.

In I Samuel 25 we read the story of Abigail. She knew who she was. She was a beautiful woman, and the Bible tells us she was an intelligent woman who had a confidence and boldness about her. She was married to a wealthy man named Nabal, who was foolish and mean and had a bad reputation. One day he was visited by David's messengers, and he insulted them, treated them badly and refused to help them. Abigail heard about the incident and was concerned for her safety and the safety of the entire household. So she bravely went straight to David and approached him and his men and offered them a peace offering. That day she spared her husband's life and those of the rest of the household. Then ten days later Nabal died of a heart attack, and not long after that David asked Abigail to be his wife. She knew who she was and she wasn't afraid to stand up for what she believed in!

Your identity is what will shape your beliefs, your thoughts, your actions and your words. So it is important to know who you are in Christ. Don't let someone else shape your beliefs for you, but you need to know what you believe and you need to know who you are in Christ.

I Peter 2:9: "But you are a chosen generation, a royal priesthood, a holy nation, His own special people, that you may proclaim the praises of Him who called you out of darkness into His marvelous light."

WEEK FORTY-FOUR

Seasons come and go

Ecclesiastes 3:1-8

To everything there is a season,
A time for every purpose under heaven:

A time to be born,
And a time to die;
A time to plant,
And a time to pluck what is planted;

A time to kill,
And a time to heal;
A time to break down,
And a time to build up;

A time to weep,
And a time to laugh;
A time to mourn,
And a time to dance;

A time to cast away stones,
And a time to gather stones;
A time to embrace,
And a time to refrain from embracing;

A time to gain,
And a time to lose;

A time to keep,
And a time to throw away;

A time to tear,
And a time to sew;
A time to keep silence,
And a time to speak;

A time to love,
And a time to hate;
A time of war,
And a time of peace.

Fall is one of my favorite seasons. When fall approaches, Asbel and I light pumpkin-scented candles, I make pumpkin bread and we drink pumpkin spice coffee. We both are huge lovers of fall weather. Spring is another season that I love because everything is starting to bloom and blossom. I can still wear a scarf and sweater because the temperatures are usually nice and cool. When I lived in Washington, DC, I would go watch the cherry blossoms along the Potomac and take lots of pictures. Everything was just beautiful and flourishing, but the blossoms don't bloom forever. They eventually go away.

The reality is we can't live in these two seasons forever. We will experience seasons that make us feel like our world is falling apart. Some winters can be brutal and can cause us to feel stranded in a blizzard (emotionally and spiritually). Then in the summer here in the south it gets so hot and humid that you can barely go outside sometimes because you can hardly breathe and it can feel as if you are in a sauna. But it's life; we will never stay in one season forever because seasons come and go.

While one is laying their loved one to rest,

154

another is bringing new life into this world.
While one is dealing with a divorce,
someone else is getting married.
While one is building a house,
someone else is trying to restore their house that has been
damaged by a flood or by a fire.

We don't have control over the seasons that come and go in our lives, . . . but we do control what and whom we lean on through each season. Choose to lean on Christ as you go through each season in life.

There is a woman in the Bible who can tell us about her season of being barren. Her name is Hannah. In I Samuel 1 we read about Hannah and her inability to have children. I am sure she felt frustrated at times and perhaps she even grew tired of waiting for spring to come to her aid. But she continued to pray and ask God for a child even through this long trial. She persevered through the winter season. One day God took her into a new season, and she had a son named Samuel, who was one of the greatest prophets in the Bible.

You may be barren and frustrated with where you are, and you may think you've missed the window of opportunity. You see everyone else's life full of joy and happiness, and they seem to be thriving. But you are sitting there barren and you feel like God has forgotten about you. (I'm talking about the dream that God gave you, the gift that you have been blessed with, the call that has become dormant, the loss you have been grieving for some time, the rejection that has pushed you into depression.)

But just know that your winter season won't last forever and that your season of being barren will soon be over! Seasons come and go.

Isaiah 60:20: "Your sun shall no longer go down,
Nor shall your moon withdraw itself;
For the LORD will be your everlasting light,
And the days of your mourning shall be ended."

WEEK FORTY-FIVE

You have more influence than you realize

In Genesis 2:17 we see that God told Adam and Eve they could eat everything in the garden but from the tree of knowledge of good and evil. They had plenty to eat and they were being taken care of, but for some reason that wasn't enough for them. In Genesis 3 Satan approached Eve and started manipulating her and began to toy with her emotions. And "boom!" she fell for it. Could it be that Satan approached Eve first because he knew how much influence she had over her husband and the future? We women play a huge role in everything that we do and in everything that we touch.

Let's look at some of the women in our world who have been influential whether it be for the good or for the bad.

Jezebel – Ahab married Jezebel (I Kings 16:31). He was the king of Israel, and her father was the king of the Zidonians and a Baal worshiper. Not long after that, Ahab started worshiping Baal, a false God. She influenced him to go further from the one God, Jehovah, and is known for being one of the most evil women during that time. What if she had told Ahab that she was serving only the One true God, Jehovah? How would their story have ended?

Mary – Jesus and His mother, Mary, were at a wedding at Cana of Galilee, and the host ran out of wine. Mary told Jesus that they had no more wine. He responded to His mother in John 2:4 (Amplified): "What is that to you and to Me? My time [to act and to be revealed] has not yet come." But Mary told the servants, "Whatever He says to you, do it." She knew her son was called to do miracles. She pushed Him to greatness

Deborah — Deborah was a prophetess and judge in Israel. Her story is told in Judges 4 and 5. She was the only woman ever to hold the position during that time. She must have kept everyone who was in a position on their toes; she was a bold woman who walked with God. One of Deborah's judgments was to instruct Barak to summon ten thousand men and attack Jabin's army. Listen to how Barak responded: "If you will go with me, then I will go; but if you will not go with me, I will not go!" (Judges 4:8). He was not willing to go into battle without her. She was a great and godly influence in that era.

My mother – She knew my father had what it took to build a great church. She was a positive voice in his life, she covered him in prayer and she believed in him. They pastored at one time over three thousand people and more, plus had fourteen daughter works (campuses). Our Easter services with all of the works were huge, and one time we even had over eight thousand in attendance. But when they were faced with difficult times, Mother would pray and fast and encourage my dad. She spoke faith when the enemy and negativity came against them, and she never cowered under pressure. She pushed him to greatness.

Don't undermine your influence as a woman in this world whether it be on the job, in the church, in your community or in your home. You can be a positive and powerful force, but it is all in how you use it. Stop being a nag, and speak life into your home and pray, fast and get into the Word. Let God affirm you, and you will stop feeling the need to have constant affirmation from others. You are a strong woman! It's all in your perspective and what you allow yourself to feed on.

Feed your soul;
Starve your insecurities!
Feed healthy relationships;
Starve unhealthy relationships!
Feed your faith ;
Starve your fears!
Feed what's important . . . starve your distractions. You can do it!
Pray for wisdom and intuition with boldness as you step into the world and make a *positive* difference.

Matthew 5:13-16: "You are the salt of the earth; but if the salt loses its flavor, how shall it be seasoned? It is then good for nothing but to be thrown out and trampled underfoot by men.

You are the light of the world. A city that is set on a hill cannot be hidden. Nor do they light a lamp and put it under a basket, but on a lampstand, and it gives light to all who are in the house. Let your light so shine before men, that they may see your good works and glorify your Father in heaven."

WEEK FORTY-SIX

Climb out of your pit

The majority of the Psalms were written from dark, depressed, wrecked and restless places. Some of the greatest songs, messages, books and ministries are created and flourishing because of a thorn that has pricked a heart, the grief someone is going through and the loneliness someone feels inside.

David wrote some of the most incredible things while in despair (Psalm 38), and at times you hear the urgency in his voice and frustration wondering where God is. Then other times you hear him praising God (Psalm 135) and seeing things in a different realm. When I read the Psalms I feel as if I could've written some of them myself, for I have been on the mountain and then I have been at a very low place in my life. But like David, I never stay there permanently, but I always seem to pull myself up out of the pit.

So today I challenge you to climb out of the pit that you find yourself in and to look toward Jesus, for it is not His will for you to stay in a depressed state for too long. I've been depressed and have thought I would never climb out of it, but one day I got tired of living in that mind-set and decided to force myself out.

Are you tired of living there? Are you ready to come out?

Change your attitude and find something to thank God for. When you start thanking Him and praising Him for your many blessings, it will change the atmosphere. Open the drapes in your bedroom, let the light in and thank God for another day. We hear a lot about speaking life nowadays. Proverbs 18:21 "Death and life are in the power of the tongue." There is something to be said about our words. We can either see the glass full or empty; it is up to us. I challenge you today to speak life into your situation and tell yourself that you will not be ruled by your circumstances any longer! You might feel stuck in the pit and being there can cause you to feel hopeless. It's almost like being stuck in a rut and a funk and you can't seem to climb out of it. But you can with God helping you. It is not His will for us to live constantly in the pit. Remember you are not the first one to find yourself in the pit and you won't be the last. You will get through this!

C. S. Lewis, the great author, lost his wife to cancer and fell to the bottom emotionally. But through that he became a passionate writer, and today you hear his quotes being used by many around the world.

Use your pain . . . use the setback in life . . . use your grief . . . use the betrayal . . . use the disappointment . . . use the diagnosis . . . use whatever you are dealing with to do something positive in life. God uses damaged people. Some of the greatest accomplishments that we read about in the Bible have been done by damaged people. He took my damaged goods and called me when I could not see anything good in my life. I had pretty much given up. But God kept me; He didn't let go! It's time to let Him take your damaged heart and ignite your dreams and passion again. It is not over! You can influence your world, your community and your circle of friends for Christ, but you have to change your attitude and refuse to stay in the pit forever.

"Turn your pit experience into a powerful and positive message."

II Samuel 22:29: "For You are my lamp, O LORD;
The LORD shall enlighten my darkness."

Date:_____

WEEK FORTY-SEVEN
You matter to God

Genesis 21:17-19
And God heard the voice of the lad. Then the angel of God
called to Hagar out of heaven, and said to her, "What ails you,
Hagar? Fear not, for God has heard the voice of the lad where
he is. Arise, lift up the lad and hold him with your hand, for I
will make him a great nation." Then God opened her eyes,
and she saw a well of water. And she went and filled the skin
with water, and gave the lad a drink.

The story of Hagar tells us a great deal about the compassion
Jesus has for people from all walks and how He wants us all
to be successful and to fulfill the call He has on our lives.
Hagar was an Egyptian, she was a servant and she was not in the tribe
of Abraham. When you have time, read the entire story about Hagar
in Genesis 16, and then in chapter 21 you will see where Sarah got rid
of Hagar. The story begins when Sarah, who was the wife of
Abraham, got tired of waiting on her promise that she would have a
child. So she persuaded Abraham to bed her servant Hagar so that she
could have a child through her. But it all backfired on Sarah. Hagar
had a son named Ishmael, and then Sarah who *should've waited on
the promise* had Isaac later in life. From that point, there was no peace
in the tribe of Abraham. Hagar despised Sarah, Sarah despised Hagar
and so the tension grew. It finally got to the point where Sarah didn't
want to share her home with Hagar and Ishmael because Isaac was

the promise and they were getting in the way. So Sarah pressured Abraham to send them away, and he did.

Sarah tossed Hagar aside like trash, but God saw Hagar as a soul who needed food, water and comfort. While Isaac and Sarah were a part of the chosen tribe of Abraham, God still had compassion on Hagar and Ishmael and took care of them.

You may think because you were not born in the right family that you don't matter. You may be working two jobs trying to survive, you may have some forgotten dreams tucked away in a folder on your shelf or you may even be the victim of a situation that you have no control over. Perhaps you are at this very moment dealing with a rejection and now struggling with not knowing where you fit in. Everyone around you seems to be passing you up and flourishing, but there you are still in the same place (so it seems). You may feel abandoned like Zion (God's people) felt in Isaiah 49:14: "The LORD has forsaken me, and my Lord has forgotten me." The Children of Israel were the apple of God's eye; He had a plan and wasn't going to forsake them even though they were in exile and being tested for their faith. It's easy to get sidetracked and forget who we are in Christ. It's easy to think we don't matter when we make bad decisions and when we don't wait on Him but instead take matters into our own hands. Yet He is still there and we still do matter to Him.

Isaiah 42:5-9 (Amplified)
He who created the heavens and stretched them out,
Who spread out the earth and its produce,
Who gives breath to the people on it
And spirit to those who walk on it,
I am the Lord, I have called You (the Messiah) in righteousness
[for a righteous purpose],

I will also take You by the hand and keep watch over You,
And I will appoint You as a covenant to the people [Israel],
As a light to the nations (Gentiles),
To open the eyes of the blind,
To bring out prisoners from the dungeon
And those who sit in darkness from the prison.
I am the Lord, that is My Name;
My glory I will not give to another,
Nor My praise to carved idols.
Indeed, the former things have come to pass,
Now I declare new things;
Before they spring forth I proclaim them to you.

You matter to God! You are in His plan!

Hagar was not born in a prestigious family, nor was she a part of the promise in Abraham's tribe. Yet God still took care of her. He told her Ishmael would have a great nation, but sadly, Ishmael made the wrong choices and destroyed his life and the promise he had over his life. Did he get bitter because he and his mother were shunned by Sarah and Abraham? Did his ego to get in the way? Did he grow tired of waiting on being a leader over a great nation? Whatever the reason, his choices destroyed the promise from taking place. He forgot who he was and became focused on his past and couldn't let it go. It doesn't matter where you come from; you still matter to God! Don't think God has forgotten about you just because it seems as if nothing is happening. God has given you life and is a God of second chances. He has given you the ability to work towards your dreams and to fulfill the call on your life. He has given you so much, but what you do with it is up to you.

WEEK FORTY-EIGHT

The burning-bush experience

While you are going through a wilderness experience, you may be dealing with some chaos and confusion in your life, but just know that God is with you. Moses was alone (so he thought) in the wilderness where it was extremely hot and dry, but God was there with him. In fact, God decided to speak to Moses in a peculiar way; He called Moses by name from a burning bush. Can you imagine if all of a sudden a bush in your yard started burning and a voice started calling your name? What would you do? I am not sure if I would stand there and have a conversation with a bush or if I would run into the house and lock the door, to be quite honest. But it happened to Moses.

Exodus 3:2, 4: "The Angel of the Lord appeared to him in a flame of fire out of the midst of a bush; and he looked, and behold, the bush burned with fire, yet was not consumed. . . . When the LORD saw that he turned aside to look, God called to him from the midst of the bush and said, 'Moses, Moses!' And he said, 'Here I am.' "

Unfortunately, the culture in which we live seems to be obsessed with *big things* and making *big splashes*, and simplicity seems to be a lost art. What if your burning experience has already been speaking to you, but you are looking for this *big wow* experience? God visited Moses when he was alone and away from the crowd. God saw something in Moses that He wanted to use. God propelled Moses later, but in the beginning it was just Moses and God.

In the last few weeks while you've been doing your devotion, praying and reading the Bible, what has God been speaking to you? Maybe He has been trying to speak to you at church, at your job or maybe even while ordering your coffee at a cafe. What has He impressed on you? Could it be that He is trying to speak to you through something as simple as that but since it wasn't big or extraordinary you dismissed it? I have found for myself that while I'm driving alone in my car, I have some of my greatest *God* moments where He speaks to me, where I write a song, a message or a thought. No one sees it; it's just me and God alone having a burning-bush moment.

Jesus didn't announce His birth with a big bang, nor were his parents invited to stay in a palace so that they could have the finest doctors and midwives to help make Mary comfortable. No! He was born in a stable, a place where animals lived. Jesus wasn't looking for a big wow moment because He was the *Big Wo*w moment! Looking through the Bible we can see many who had their personal burning-bush experiences. Since there are too many to name, I've decided to list just a few:

- Mary the mother of Jesus – An angel visited her in a dream and told her she had found favor with God. There she had a burning-bush experience where she was told she that was with child and that He would be the Son of God, the Savior of the world. She was never the same after that (Luke 1:26-38).

- Saul, who later became the apostle Paul – He was on his way to destroy the disciples of Christ in Damascus, but on his way a bright light from heaven flashed around him and he fell to the ground. There the Lord began speaking to him, and in Acts 9:5: "And he said, 'Who are You, Lord?' Then the Lord said, 'I am Jesus, whom you are persecuting.' " Saul was never the same after that; he became one of the most influential men during that era for Jesus.

- Peter – He was a fisherman living a normal life when Jesus approached him and told him to follow Him. It was a simple request, and in that moment Peter gave up his personal agenda and dreams and became a disciple of Christ. A simple burning-bush moment changed him so that he was never the same afterward (Mark 1:16-17).

- Mary Magdalene, a prostitute – She had a burning-bush experience when Jesus set her free and delivered her from demonic spirits. It was a defining moment in her life, and she followed Jesus and did His will for the rest of her life (Luke 8:1-3).

What burning-bush experience have you had and maybe you have not viewed it as one because you were looking for something bigger to make its grand entrance? He can speak to you through something simple. Perhaps it's time to stop limiting God and to realize that He is the BIG even in the small things.

Jeremiah 33:3 (Amplified): "Call to Me and I will answer you, and tell you [and even show you] great and mighty things, [things which have been confined and hidden], which you do not know and understand and cannot distinguish."

WEEK FORTY-NINE

Be intentional

I Timothy 4:15-16:
"Meditate on these things; give yourself entirely to them, that your progress may be evident to all. Take heed to yourself and to the doctrine. Continue in them, for in doing this you will save both yourself and those who hear you."

There is a song that I love by Travis Greene, called "Intentional." The first part of the song goes like this.

"All things working for my good
He's intentional
Never failing
I know that all things are working for my good
He's intentional
Never failing."

Jesus is intentional about the plan He has for our lives. He is intentional about molding us and shaping us into the people He wants us to be. He is intentional about our fulfilling His purpose in our lives. But are we being intentional about our own lives, our attitudes and our dreams, and are we being intentional about fulfilling His purpose? When we are living intentionally it means that we are taking responsibility for our mental, emotional, spiritual and physical well-being. This means how we respond to things that come in and out of our lives. All of us have a desire to do something, we all have dreams, we all have goals and we all want to do our passion, but the question is, "Are you being intentional about it?"

It's easy for us to get inspired and to draft a plan and set a timeline for it to be executed, but following through and being intentional about it can be challenging. Usually it's just plain old life that gets in the way, and then sometimes we allow people's opinions to cause us to second-guess our intentions and dreams. We then find ourselves vacillating that maybe we didn't hear from God or maybe it's just too much work or maybe we missed the window of opportunity. If God is in it, it doesn't matter how many windows of opportunity you miss. He will open the door when it's time. Seek His will for your life as you become intentional about your dreams.

What do you need to be more intentional about?

1. *Morning devotions* (prayer, mediating, studying the Bible, focusing on His plan for your life)

2. *Exercise* (walking, running, biking, and cardio. It's all good for the mind, body and soul)

3. *Eating healthy* (protein, fruits, vegetables, nuts) Then eat chocolate! ☺ I am a chocoholic.

4. *Sending a card* (to a friend, a spouse, a parent, a sibling, a co-worker, somebody who needs encouragement)

5. *Working towards a dream* (Don't stop working towards it even if you have to take a break from it. Don't allow anyone to talk you out of something that God has put in your heart. Don't give up on it)

6. *Being more sensitive to those around you* (someone may be going through a divorce, facing a terminal disease, feeling lonely, grieving a loss, battling depression)

7. *Investing in the right relationships* (put your energy into the right relationships and build trust, security and a bond that goes deep)

8. *Taking time to rest your mind* (take a break from your normal schedule, go read a book, get a coffee and just sit, sit outside and enjoy the mountains or the beach (if it's within reach) or just stay home and shut out the noise)

9. *Protect your heart* (Set healthy boundaries in your relationships, don't allow yourself to be a doormat for someone to constantly step on and use. It's okay to say no when necessary; be vigilant with what you allow yourself to feed on and to listen to.)

10. *Protect your integrity* (Be honest in business and in relationships; be ethical in everything you do. People may not see everything behind the scenes, but God sees everything that we do.)

These are just a few things I jotted down that I think all of us can relate to. Jesus is being intentional and working for our good, so let's be intentional about our own lives and work towards being the people we desire to be . . . for Him.

"The quality of your commitments will determine the course of your life."

— Ralph Marston

MONDAY MORNINGS with Stephenie

WEEK FIFTY

Show a little mercy

Luke 6:36: "Therefore be merciful, just as your Father also is merciful."

"I have always found that mercy bears richer fruits than strict justice."

— Abraham Lincoln

We are sometimes harder on those who do things that we cannot even fathom doing ourselves. It is not our struggle; therefore, we can tend not to show mercy like we should. In fact, we get out the ruler and start measuring the sin in others. Yes, we need to stand strong, but at the same time we need to extend mercy to all. I have been guilty of judging others and assuming things about people, and sadly, I have not always shown mercy. We are probably all guilty of categorizing sins sometimes, as in putting one sin above another when in fact sin is sin, period!

I have learned never to say, "I would never do what they did" or "My child would never do that; that is just horrible" or "that would never happen in my home." Please come off the pedestal and realize that it is by God's grace and mercy that you've never done that or that your child or spouse has never done *that* horrible sin. We get so caught up in our religious traditions and piety that we don't realize that we are just a prayer away from messing up too. We are human and never know when something will hit our home and bring devastation to us. Oh, that we might show more mercy towards the fallen! Oh, that we might extend love to those who are broken! Oh, that we might show compassion to those who are not like us! Oh, that we might pray and weep for those who find themselves in a web of failures and sin!

Where would I be had my parents not loved me back to Jesus? What if they would've shunned me and told me I was an embarrassment to them and their legacy? I was a prodigal wounded and, yes, I did some things I am not proud of, but my soul was more important to them! My parents were more concerned about my soul than they were about what people thought. They prayed for me, fasted for my soul and loved me back. It didn't happen overnight. I had left God and Christianity for over five years, but Dad and Mom showed me mercy through that season. (I can tell you that even when someone seems as if she doesn't care about God or your unconditional love and you reaching out to them, she does. I was one of those people. There were times I would get home at 3 AM from being out and would cry myself to sleep and ask Jesus to heal my heart. I wasn't even going to church nor did I want to go, but I had those moments where I was tender and knew that I needed God to do surgery on my heart.)

Something jaded me even more during that time. It was rumors. I heard all kinds of things, and it broke my heart even more. Some of them were assumptions, made-up stories and pure gossip, but the Bible is very clear about destroying other people with gossip. I was already down, but some were so out of tune with the condition of my heart and continued to shoot arrows and wounded me even more. Don't kick someone down when he is already down, and please don't shoot the wounded more than he has already been wounded. It might be you one day or it might be your child or someone close to you. Show mercy and kindness and pray for the wandering. We need a baptism of mercy in the church today. We need to become in sync with God's heartbeat and passion for the world around us.

Proverbs 6:16-19
"These six things the LORD hates,
Yes, seven are an abomination to Him:
A proud look,
A lying tongue,
Hands that shed innocent blood,
A heart that devises wicked plans,
Feet that are swift in running to evil,
A false witness who speaks lies,
And one who sows discord among brethren."

We hurt people when we assume things and when we allow a rumor to trump a person's soul. Who wants to go to a place where stones are being thrown? We need to be more sensitive and in tune and prayerful for people who are broken and hurting. If you are concerned about someone, pray for her and weep for where she is in life. Ask Jesus to let you see through His eyes when you look at people. I have found myself praying for God to give me more compassion and mercy towards people in general. We live in a world that is very hateful, insensitive and angry, but we in the church should not be hateful and angry because we serve a different God. We serve Jesus Christ! We are not of this world, so we shouldn't act like this world!

Perhaps you are reading this with tears running down your cheeks because you are wounded; maybe you are a minister's child who has walked away from church or maybe you know someone close to you who has been wounded and wants nothing to do with Christianity. You may even sing on the praise team every Sunday at church, but you are faking your smile and acting as if everything is okay but it is not okay. You are tired of wearing a mask but you can't bear the thought of being the brunt of someone's criticism, so you find it easier to pretend. Maybe you are guilty of gossiping about others and one who has a hard time extending mercy. You have put yourself on the throne and judge everyone who doesn't live up to your standards. It's time to get off of the throne, for there is only one God who is the judge. He doesn't need our help judging. Instead of judging others and making it your business to put people in their place, why don't you start praying for them and why don't you reach out to them? Why don't you show some mercy because one day you may need mercy yourself? Stop killing people spiritually and get a burden for people who need healing and restoration. We the church have got to get to a place where we feel sadness when we hear about someone's sins, failures and mistakes. We need to get to a place where we weep for the things that makes God weep. May God give the church a burden for prodigals and for people in general, and may we pray for them. If we the church can't show mercy and God's love, who is going to do it? Time is of essence; God is coming soon. It is time to pray for the wounded and broken people in our circle, community and world.

Lamentations 3:40: "Let us search out and examine our ways, And turn back to the LORD."

May we see through His eyes and search our own hearts.

WEEK FIFTY-ONE

You are safe under His wings

Psalm 91:4
He shall cover you with His feathers,
And under His wings you shall take refuge;
His truth shall be your shield and buckler.

P salm 91 happens to be one of my favorite passages in the entire Bible. When I was in fifth grade our teacher had our class memorize it, and I have never forgotten it. It seems that I find myself quoting it more and more as I face the reality that nothing is safe apart from Him, but I can hide under His wings because He is my refuge and my God in whom I trust.

There is something significant about hiding under His wings.

"Keep me as the apple of the eye, hide me under the shadow of thy wings" (Psalm 17:8, KJV).

"How excellent is thy lovingkindness, O God! therefore the children of men put their trust under the shadow of thy wings" (Psalm 36:7, KJV).

Some birds, when defending their young, put their own bodies between them and the danger that is trying to get to them. The mother will stand in the gap for her babies no matter the cost. In fact, a mother hen, when she sees a hawk flying overhead, spreads her wings and start clucking. Her little chicks scurry to safety under her wings. Then she draws her wings in, covering her little chicks. She is telling the hawk that to get to her little chicks, it would have to come through her first. She is willing to lay down her life for her chicks. This is how Jesus feels about us. He laid down His life for us and is willing to fight for us. He desires to cover us with His wings. If you need rest, run to Him. If you need shelter from the rain, run to Him. If you need a healing, run to Him. If you need protection from your enemies, run to Him. If you need peace and calm in your life, run to Him and let His wings cover you.

When you are under His wings, He will protect you and He will guide you and give you strength. When you are under His wings, He will be with you through your dark nights and will turn your weeping into laughter. Let Him cover you with His wings and take you to places that you thought were impossible. Under His wings there is safety, restoration and everlasting love.

Psalm 91

He who dwells in the secret place of the Most High
Shall abide under the shadow of the Almighty.
I will say of the Lord, "He is my refuge and my fortress;
My God, in Him I will trust."
Surely He shall deliver you from the snare of the fowler]
And from the perilous pestilence.
He shall cover you with His feathers,
And under His wings you shall take refuge;
His truth shall be your shield and buckler.
You shall not be afraid of the terror by night,
Nor of the arrow that flies by day,
Nor of the pestilence that walks in darkness,
Nor of the destruction that lays waste at noonday.

A thousand may fall at your side,
And ten thousand at your right hand;
But it shall not come near you.
Only with your eyes shall you look,
And see the reward of the wicked.
Because you have made the Lord, who is my refuge,
Even the Most High, your dwelling place,   .
No evil shall befall you,
Nor shall any plague come near your dwelling;
For He shall give His angels charge over you,
To keep you in all your ways.
In their hands they shall bear you up,
Lest you dash your foot against a stone.
You shall tread upon the lion and the cobra,
The young lion and the serpent you shall trample underfoot.
Because he has set his love upon Me, therefore I will deliver him;
I will set him on high, because he has known My name.
He shall call upon Me, and I will answer him;
I will be with him in trouble;
I will deliver him and honor him.

With long life I will satisfy him,
And show him My salvation."

WEEK FIFTY-TWO

Most women carry a secret

Most women carry a secret
Are you one of those women
Who has suffered in silence
Who has had regrets
Who has had to deal with the red flags in life that ended up
tearing you apart inside.
Who has cried in private and then smiled in public pretending
everything was fine
Who has been hurt and has had to deal with a difficult
curveball in life
Who has put others before her
Who has wanted to just run away from life
Who has wanted to just let your hair down and act like a little girl
Who has crumbled emotionally but held it together on the outside
Who has been forced to lay aside a dream but nearly every
week you think about it
Who has made some bad choices
Who feels there is no fire left inside to do anything
Who has become calloused to the things around you
Who has a hard time trusting others
Who has tossed the call aside because it just got too hard
Who has a sensitive heart but comes across as hard person
Who just wants to feel again
Who won't let anyone get too close

Who just wants to be free from the guilt you have been
carrying for a long time
Who has some skeletons in the closet and you are fearful that
someone will find out
Who wants to love again, really love again
Who wants to be loved, romanced, really loved and
romanced again.
Who everyone leans on and calls the strong one but you need
someone to lean on yourself

What is your secret today that no one knows about that you have
kept hidden from others. Those tears that you quickly wipe away so no
one will see. God sees them, He knows what is going on inside. We can
hide it from others but we can never hide it from God. Let Him caress
your heart today and hold you. He wants the best for you, He really does!
Take your heart to Jesus and tell Him how you feel. Write your thoughts
down in prayer mode if you have to but talk to Him....God knows the
secrets that lie within your soul. Give it to Him today. Let Him stir up
the gifts inside you, revive you, and restore you today.

Psalm 71:20 "You who have shown me many troubles
and distresses.
Will revive and renew me again,
And will bring me up again from the depths of the earth."

God sees where you are, He is more powerful than your secrets,
He is more powerful than your dilemma. You may be fighting for
your life and your home. Call on the name of Jesus, and let Him
fight your battles! You are a warrior in His army. You are not just
the average woman on the street, but you have something inside you
that is powerful: Jesus Christ! We win the battle through prayer, so

don't look at the circumstances but look at the God of your circumstances. There is something about the power of prayer that we women need to do more of. When all hell breaks loose in your life, go to prayer and talk to God about it. He will answer in the time of trouble, so don't give up!

Psalm 107:28-30
"Then they cry out to the LORD in their trouble,
And He brings them out of their distresses.
He calms the storm,
So that its waves are still.
Then they are glad because they are quiet;
So He guides them to their desired haven."

I challenge all women to never give up!

I challenge all women to persevere through the fire!

I challenge all women to pray and to fast!

I challenge all women to take control over your thoughts!

I challenge all women to walk in His will for your life!

I challenge all women to stop letting the enemy make you feel defeated!

I challenge all women to get some fire in your belly and to fight on!

I challenge all women to not allow insecurity to drive you!

I challenge all women to not let depression keep you down!

I challenge all women to move forward like David and start killing the Goliath's in your life once and for all!

Refuse to give up!

I challenge you to give God your secrets and to march forward!